Pirates, Raiders & Invaders of the Gulf Coast

Pirates, Raiders & Invaders of the Gulf Coast

RYAN STARRETT &
JOSH FOREMAN

THE
History
PRESS

Published by The History Press
Charleston, SC
www.historypress.com

First published 2023

Manufactured in the United States

ISBN 9781467153232

Library of Congress Control Number: 2023937165

To Joseph Padraic and Penelope Rose O.: thank you for your request that I write a book on one of your many avocations: pirates. Your entreaty led us all along the Gulf Coast, from the pirate museums in St. Augustine to Galveston, and a score of adventures in between.

To the memory of Mike Leach: "Swing your sword!"

CONTENTS

Preface

DRAMATIS PERSONAE

THE INDIANS: As transients themselves, the Gulf Coastal tribes fought for land and security. Not under any centralized authority, the Indians were the most fragmented of the actors. For example, there is no Creek Nation. Instead, there are various Creek clans, and within each clan, there are varying factions. As a whole, the Indians fought for a homeland—stability, hunting grounds and an advantage over their rivals.

THE BLACKS: The first Black people brought to the Gulf Coast were familiar with slavery, having lived with the institution in Africa and having been sold by fellow African rulers. The second, third and fourth generations came to realize that their slavery was to be generational, with its concomitant combination of hopelessness and perseverance. Some accepted their fate with a quiet will to exist, to live, to endure. Others chose to resist, sometimes by force of arms.

THE FRENCH: Denied the wealth of Mexico and the tobacco- and rice-rich lands of the Atlantic coast, the French turned their attention to Canada and the interior. The demand for furs ensured continued French interest in the Americas. In possession of Canada (at least until 1763), the French sought a southern outlet for their northern and inland warehouses. A Gulf Coast presence, along with control of the Mississippi River, would ensure a depot for their goods and keep them competitive in the Gulf Coast game of thrones.

THE BRITISH: Initially excluded from the lands of the Gulf, the British found themselves embroiled in coastal politics after the conclusion of the French and Indian War in 1763, when His Britannic Majesty acquired East and West Florida. Twenty years later, after losing half their American colonies to revolution, the British considered themselves fortunate to continue to hold their far more valuable sugar colonies. To the British, the oft-neglected Gulf Coast was only a bargaining chip or buffer for their island colonies…unless New Orleans fell into their orbit.

THE SPANISH: God, gold, glory…and a buffer zone protecting the mines of Mexico. Spanish policy revolved around protecting the riches of its richest provinces. Too many ships carrying the treasures of empire were lost on their way to Spain. So much more treasure-rich land was at risk of foreign invasion. A presence along the Gulf Coast—along with a clever manipulation of Indian tribes—would ensure the survival of Havana and Mexico City.

THE AMERICANS: Operating under the assumption that God had tasked the "City Upon a Hill" with the subjugation of a continent, the *Norteamericanos* spread across North America like a downward right hand unfurling to the west and thumb to the south. The Americans intended to repay the exorbitant cost of their independency with land—land they would conquer from the Atlantic to the Pacific to the Gulf of Mexico…and perhaps beyond.

THE RENEGADES: Outlaws? Opportunists? Nationalists? The renegades of the Gulf sought what nearly everyone was seeking: livelihood and money. They just sought it outside the law. Whether squatters, filibusters, revolutionaries, privateers or pirates; whether Indian, Black, European or any mixture of them; whether desperate, clever, manipulative, opportunistic or patriotic, the renegades of the Gulf became some of the region's most colorful and controversial—and at times powerful—figures.

INTRODUCTION

No other land in the United States has been as contested as the Mississippi Gulf Coast. In just 120 years, from 1699 to 1819, the flags of six nations flew over the region: Spain, France, Great Britain, Muskogee, the West Florida Republic and the United States. And this list does not include the various Indian tribes who vied for control of valuable hunting grounds, nor the slave rebellions and Maroon colonies initiated and established by Africans and their descendants seeking freedom.

The Gulf was a region that the pre-contact tribes believed was better visited than occupied. It was a region of scarcity and danger. Because of the incessant winds, the trees grew smaller, and the animals were less abundant. It was not a land conducive to farming. True, the sea and sound provided ample food, but proximity to the sea also brought hurricanes and deadly storms. The Mississippi Gulf Coast is a land of the hardened, a land of survivors.

It is also a land of unspeakable wealth—now and in the early colonial period. Pensacola possesses one of the preeminent harbors of the Gulf Coast. Mobile and Biloxi provide their own harbors and ports, control of which meant control of the bountiful natural resources of the Southeast's drainage basins and watersheds. Galveston, now a popular tourist destination and shipping hub, was once the capital of the Republic of Texas and then the site of the emancipation of the nation's last slaves on June 19, 1865.[1] And then there is New Orleans, the mighty Mississippi River's southernmost port, where untold riches empty into the Gulf to be shipped across the world. Control of New Orleans meant control of the Mississippi River. So important was the Crescent City that Thomas Jefferson remarked, "There is on the globe one single spot, the possessor of which is our natural and habitual enemy. It is New Orleans, through which the produce of three eighths of our territory must pass to market."[2]

Not only did the Gulf Coast control the harbors and rivers to its north, but its cultural and economic influence also reached north and inward to Baton Rouge, Natchez and Tallahassee and from west to east, from Galveston to St. Marks. Control of the Gulf Coast meant control of the fur trade. It meant control of tariffs. It meant control of a region.

And so, seven distinctive "peoples" fought to raise their standards over the land, from midden mounds to old-world heraldic emblems to various stars and stripes. Control of the Gulf Coast meant wealth and security. It meant empire.

Chapter 1

THE FRENCH AND INDIAN WARS, 1702–1759

THE FRENCH

1702, Mobile
Pierre Le Moyne d'Iberville

Pierre Le Moyne d'Iberville made his way to the fort at La Mobile, where he hoped to engineer his greatest coup to date by establishing peace between his colony's two bitterest and most powerful—the Choctaws and Chickasaws.

Iberville believed that only through peace could he ensure the success of Louisiana. Only by uniting the Indians could he resist the English. Peace between the Choctaws and Chickasaws would give France security and mastery of the Gulf Coast.

Standing in the way of peace was the ancient animosity between the two peoples—and the English, who stood to profit from internecine war. War meant profit for those who possessed war materiel—profit for officers, but mostly, profit for the slavers.

The Carolina English and their Indian allies had overhunted the deer and beaver populations. They adapted by focusing on a plantation economy fueled by rice and indigo, but the growing eastern plantations required slaves. By encouraging war and arming their Chickasaw allies, the English were not only equipping their farms with captured slaves but also weakening

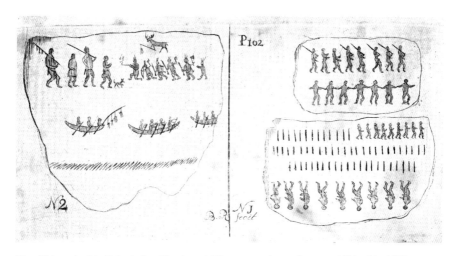

Two "hieroglyphics" depicting Creek and Choctaw actions of war, published in 1775.
Beinecke Library at Yale University.

the French, who hoped to exploit the still abundant fur trade south and west of the English colonies. Iberville's mission was to put an end to the Indian wars that benefited only the English.[3]

ON APRIL 11, 1702, after an exploratory voyage inland, Iberville returned to his fort in La Mobile. Awaiting him were letters from the Spanish commandant in Pensacola, who was again requesting provisions from the French for his own starving citizens. Awaiting him was the rain that had been falling for days—rain that would follow for days to come and fill the nearly finished powder magazine, causing it to collapse. Awaiting him was the starved and ghostly master tanner who had been lost and, after two weeks, found standing in front of a self-dug grave and a cross on which he had written his story. But of paramount concern to Iberville was the absence of the Choctaw and Chickasaw chiefs on whom the future of his colony depended. He would spend the next two suspenseful weeks awaiting their arrival.

At last, three Chickasaw and four Choctaw chiefs arrived for the most important meeting in Louisiana's brief history. The two delegations arrived simultaneously, were greeted by Iberville and told that the council would commence in the morning.[4]

March 26, 1702

At eight o'clock in the morning, the French, Choctaws and Chickasaws met in council. Iberville began by distributing gifts to the two factions. He then turned the meeting over to his younger brother, Jean-Baptiste Le Moyne d'Bienville. The muscular Frenchman—a son of Montreal, accustomed to the fineries of a privileged life, charming and courtly but who had learned several native dialects,[5] traveled large swaths of the Gulf Coast and bore numerous tattoos both Catholic and Indian beneath his tunic—stood before the seven chiefs and translated for Iberville:

> *I rejoice to live to see you disposed to live in peace with each other and with all the nations of the region…. The Chickasaw have foolishly followed the advice of the English, who have no other objective than to work their destruction by inciting the Chickasaw and the Choctaw to make war on each other so the English can get slaves, whom they send away to other countries to be sold.*[6]

To hammer home his point, Iberville pointed out that the English had bought Chickasaw captives from an enemy tribe. A true ally would have returned their friends to their village. Instead, the traders sold the captured Chickasaws to a Caribbean island far away. Bienville continued to translate:

> *You Chickasaw can observe that during the last eight to ten years when you have been at war with the Choctaw, at the instigation of the English, who gave you ammunition and thirty guns for that purpose, you have taken more than 500 prisoners and killed more than 1,800 Choctaw. Those prisoners were sold; but taking those prisoners cost you more than 800 men, slain on various war parties, who would be living at this moment if it had not been for the English. The Choctaw see it well—and the Chickasaw ought to see it, too—that the Englishman is to blame for the loss of your dead brothers. And the ultimate plan of the Englishman, after weakening you by means of wars, is to come and seize you in your villages and then send you away to be sold somewhere else, in faraway countries from which you can never return, as the English have treated others, as you know. To prevent these calamities, you must no longer listen to the Englishman.*[7]

After first appealing to their reason, Iberville turned to threats. Unless the Chickasaws expelled the English from their villages, Iberville would cease

JEAN BAPTISTE LE MOYNE DE BIENVILLE.

Left: Jean Baptiste le Moyne de Bienville. *Library of Congress.*

Right: Portrait of a Chickasaw man, taken in 1876. *Beinecke Library at Yale University.*

to trade with them. Instead, he would continue to arm his own allies—and their enemy—the Choctaws. Furthermore, he would begin to arm his other allies hostile to the Chickasaws, namely the Natchez and the Mobilians. Perhaps deadliest of all, he would incite the Illinois tribes loyal to France to make war on the Chickasaw:

> *Certainly you see that you will be in no condition to hold out against so many nations; you will suffer the sorrow of seeing yourselves killed at the gates of your villages, along with your women and children.*[8]

After waving the stick, Iberville offered the carrot. Should the Chickasaws drive the English traders from their villages and make peace with the Choctaws, he promised to build a trading post between the two peoples and provide French trade goods in exchange for "skins of buffalo, bear and deer—those are the slaves I want. You will feed yourselves and all your families on the meat of the animals you kill. To get them will not cost you your lives."[9] He also pledged to return Chickasaw prisoners who had been captured by the Illinois.

The two peoples, Choctaws and Chickasaws, agreed to Iberville's proposal. After distributing hooded cloaks, rifles and "trinkets" to the chiefs, the French commander prepared to set sail for France. It would be Iberville's third voyage from the New World to the Old. It would be his last.

Behind him, peace had been established along the Gulf Coast. It would not last long.

The Indians

1716, near Grand Village
The Natchez

The Frenchmen were growing rapacious. Their presence was spreading along the Coast, and their influence was gradually pushing north. They had an established warehouse in the central village and were threatening to connect their holdings in the Illinois territory with those of the Gulf. Furthermore, the English had become a viable alternative. Their goods were cheaper and better made.

And so, when four French traders made their way up the Mississippi River, the Bearded One, chief of the Jenzenacque village, decided to act. The four traders were killed and dumped in the river.

Unfortunately for the Great Sun, chief of Grand Village and the highest ranking of the six Natchez chiefs, one of the Frenchmen in his village noticed the slain men's goods scattered among several Natchez warriors as booty. The Frenchman quietly alerted his superior.

And so began a chain of events that would, in fifteen short years, lead to the de facto extinction of the Natchez people. The six Natchez villages were already divided in their response to the encroaching Europeans, with some favoring English traders and others French. That one faction or the other would win out had become inevitable, for the Europeans had unleashed an arms race. To compete with hostile surrounding tribes—whether they be Choctaws, Chickasaws, Tunicas or one of the countless other tribes of the Gulf region and Mississippi Valley—the Natchez needed guns. And when their enemies acquired a shipment of guns, they needed more and more and more. And then they needed a constant supply of powder and bullets, the blacksmiths to fix the guns when they broke and more powder and bullets and guns to shoot more deer to trade for more guns. And when the price of

"Indians employed in planting corn." Taken from a 1564 drawing by Jacob le Moyne. *Library of Congress.*

pelts dropped, they needed more guns to shoot more deer to trade for more guns to protect themselves from their enemies who were in the process of buying more guns. In short, the English and French traders had become an evil necessity. Only one question remained: which side to choose?

Soon after, another French trading expedition on its way to Illinois arrived among the Natchez of Grand Village. The fifteen-man expedition exchanged the customary pleasantries with the Natchez aristocracy and requested guides.

The Great Sun appointed eight guides to accompany the vessel. When word reached the Bearded One at Jenzenacque, he set out with 150 warriors to a turn in the river, intent on capturing the boat, dispatching the traders and plundering the merchandise. Unfortunately for the Natchez coffers, one of the guides betrayed the plot to one of the Frenchmen, Andre Penicaut, before the boat reached the site of the ambush. The other seven guides likewise confessed the plot. Rewarded with trade goods, the guides accompanied the Frenchmen back toward Grand Village.

When the expedition and their guides neared their point of departure, Penicaut entered the village alone, claiming to have fallen ill along the way. The Great Sun placed him in a house with the only Frenchman who had remained behind to keep an eye on the warehouse. He placed three Natchez warriors in the same house. The following morning, the two Frenchmen were gone. The furious chief ordered the warehouse seized.

When one of the Natchez chiefs learned that the Frenchmen had escaped to the neighboring Tunicas to the south, he sent a delegation to convince the Tunica chief to kill the traders—and the missionary priest residing among them for good measure. Writing his memoir decades later, Andre Penicaut blamed the Great Sun for the attempted assassinations. Penicault, however, made the mistake that most Europeans made when dealing with the Indians: they assumed that the different tribes existed as independent nation states—without the legal status, of course. In other words, the Great Sun, the highest-ranking Natchez chief, spoke for all Natchez tribes, in the same way that a European governor or general would speak for his nation as a whole. But the fact of the matter is that the Gulf Coast tribes operated more along the lines of a confederacy, where each village operated independently. The various villages tended to work together for mutual protection, but they were not obligated to follow a central authority. In fact, during the Natchez War of 1716, the six villages were divided down the middle, with the Grand Village, Tioux and Flour siding with the French and the Grigra, Jenzenacque and White Earth or White Apple with the British.[10]

The Great Sun (or whichever chief attempted to orchestrate the assassinations), having promised to join the Tunicas in war against the French, was disappointed in the morning when his three delegates returned and reported that they had barely returned with their own lives, and only because of the intervention of the priest. The French, by now, were no doubt safely on their way to Mobile. The war that at least some of the chiefs had hoped for would soon be upon them.

Not long after, a French trader named Richard was sailing down from Illinois, ignorant of recent developments. Natchez warriors captured the unwary Frenchman, confiscated his wares, brought him back to their village, chopped off his hands and feet and tossed him in a mud pit.[11] French retaliation was now inevitable.

The Natchez chiefs soon learned that Jean-Baptiste Le Moyne d'Bienville was marching north at the head of fifty French soldiers and a three-month supply of food and materiel. Presently, the French were encamped on an island in the Mississippi River, surrounded by a hastily erected stockade. When a French interpreter entered the Natchez village and requested a parley back at their own stockade, the Great Sun acquiesced and agreed to attend and meet the feared leader of the French, who threatened to be either an implacable enemy or a father to the Natchez (a most curious boon considering the Natchez were a matrilineal society where the mother's brother was the most important male influence to a newborn boy).[12] The Great Sun and his two younger brothers, Tattooed Serpent and Little Sun, as well as the Bearded One and three other village chiefs, prepared to negotiate with the French commander.

About a week before the Natchez delegation set off for the island, six Canadian traders were captured on the river and brought to the Bearded One's Jenzenaque village along the Natchez Trace and next to the ancient Emerald Mound. For three days, the Natchez debated what to do with the Frenchmen as the people broke into two camps, pro-English and pro-French. In the end, the latter faction won out, and the Canadians were released. They immediately and gratefully made their way to Bienville's island stockade with their story.[13]

When the Natchez arrived at the island palisade a few days later, they began preparations to smoke the calumet.[14] Bienville refused and arrested the entire delegation, including the Great Sun, justifying himself because, as Penicaut explained, "it is always necessary to be suspicious of savages, who are greatly addicted to betrayal of their word."[15] Bienville said that they would be released only when the blood price of the five murdered French traders was paid. He demanded the culprits' heads, chief among whom was the uncle of the Great Sun, the recently captured Bearded One.

The Great Sun's younger brother Tattooed Serpent agreed to carry out the executions, but he was deemed too valuable a hostage. Instead, the youngest brother, Little Sun, was set free to exact French vengeance on his people.

Less than a week later, Little Sun returned with three heads—two of the murderers and the head of the brother of a third murderer whom Little Sun could not locate. (The French had learned that a scalp could be deceptive; a head could not, due to the distinctive Natchez tattoo marks.)[16] The French commander's request made little sense. Disputes were waged between groups, not individuals. A certain number of Frenchmen had been slain. The same number of Natchez heads were paid in exchange.[17] Little Sun had assumed that since wars occurred between peoples, the head of a brother would suffice. Bienville, however, was aghast at the murder of an innocent man. The fact that Little Sun also brought back a Frenchman who had been captured by pro-English Natchez just days before and had been sentenced to death by burning did not assuage Bienville's anger. The Frenchman had Little Sun thrown back in prison.

Shooting a Woodcock, by Charles Jacque (1864). *Metropolitan Museum of Art.*

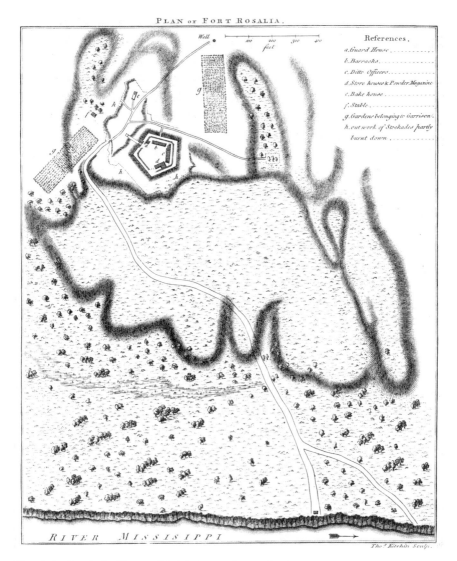

Plan of Fort Rosalia, by Thomas Kitchin (1770). *Internet Archive.*

Not long after, the island began to flood. Still, Bienville remained and held on to his prisoners. Makeshift lodging was built just above the waters, and Bienville brought the three brothers to his own lodging. There he ascertained more clearly the dynamics of the civil conflict raging in the Natchez community. Having been on the cramped and flooded island for a month and with no end to the stalemate in sight, Bienville offered a deal to the three brothers: assent to the execution of the two pro-British chiefs imprisoned on the island (including their uncle, the Bearded One), execute the other pro-British chief should he ever return to any Natchez village and construct a fort 150 feet by 90 feet on the bluffs overlooking the Mississippi River, where the French would maintain a warehouse and garrison indefinitely.

With a civil war looming among the Natchez, with those along the Great River favoring the French and those closer to the Natchez Trace the English, the Great Sun had little choice but to acquiesce to Bienville's demands. With the British providing their allies with desperately needed muskets and balls—including half the Natchez villages, as well as the Chickasaw—the Great Sun entered the arms race on the side of the French. The price? A French fort in the midst of his autonomous village. And the death of his uncle.

The Bearded One and the pro-English chief of the Grigra settlement were summarily dispatched. An eyewitness recorded the scene:

> *The Bearded ceased for a moment singing his death song and sang that of war. He related his great deeds against different nations and the number of scalps he had carried away. He named the five Frenchmen he had caused to die, and said that he died with regret at not having killed more. The Tattooed Serpent, who was then the only one of his nation among us, listened attentively and said to M. de Bienville, "He is my brother, but I do not regret him. You are ridding us of a bad man."* [18]

And so, the leaders of the pro-English faction of the Natchez were either dead or exiled. The "Sun" brothers were back in power. A strong fort stood just outside the spiritual center at Grand Village. The Natchez had tied their fate to the French. In thirteen years, the folly of that decision would lead to the largest massacre of Europeans in North America and the destruction of one of the Gulf Coast's most historic and powerful tribes. [19]

The Renegades

1744–1757, New Orleans to Havana
Jean Baptiste Baudreau II

Jean Baptiste Baudreau II, the son of a landed French gentleman and his Choctaw mistress, sailed his sloop into Mobile Bay. He had just concluded another successful run to Pensacola, unloaded his contraband and returned to his wife, Marie Catherine Vinconneau. He also returned to his lover, Henriette Huet, whose family owned a nearby plantation.

Unbeknownst to the smuggler, Governor Vaudreuil of New Orleans had sent the commandant of Mobile a warning: the "half-breed" Jean Baptiste was smuggling "refreshments"[20] to the Spanish at Pensacola and must be stopped:

> *As for Baudrau, who seems to have already violated our regulations, not just once but repeatedly in going there without permission, he should be punished by you as an example to others. You should order him to report to you and explain his behavior. This having been done, you should detain him, sir, eight days in your prison for his first lesson and, in the event of a repeat offense, you should hold him until you receive further instructions from me.*[21]

Jean Baptiste had made one too many successful runs with his bootleg merchandise. He had also made one too many trysts with Henriette, who was now pregnant. With a smuggling charge hanging over his head like the sword of Damocles, and now with two future charges likely pending—fathering

Guercino, the Prisoner, by Philip Henry Delamotte (circa 1855). *Rijksmuseum.*

a bastard child and seducing a minor—Jean Baptiste was short on options. So was Henriette. Pregnant by a mixed-race smuggler and about to lose her inheritance to her crafty brother-in-law, Ignace Petit, Henriette begged Jean Baptiste to elope. The couple stole a boat and provisions from the Huet house and convinced three slaves to flee with them.[22]

An infuriated Petit charged Jean Baptiste with robbing the Huet home and kidnapping the daughter. His friend Vaudreuil immediately sent a dispatch to Mobile:

> *You ought to send Mr. Ballu in search of Baudro right away. I have sent some Indians to see if he is near Chandeleur Island, as it has been rumored here. When I know his whereabouts for certain, I will have him arrested.*[23]

The governor also sent letters to Pensacola, St. Marks and Havana warning of the dangerous renegade, the kidnapped and the three runaways. Soon after disembarking at Havana, the elopers were arrested and returned to New Orleans, Henriette to her brother-in-law, the slaves to their owner and Jean Baptiste to prison, where he was sentenced to ten years as a galley slave.

October 25, 1744

As a man acclimated to the freedom of the Gulf, at ease in the woods with his mother's relations and the son of a father of the colony, Jean Baptiste had no intention of being shackled to the oar of a ship. During the night of October 25, 1744, Jean Baptiste and two Englishmen cut their iron chains, and at three o'clock in the morning, they lowered themselves by rope from the prison window. They ran as far as they could until sunrise forced them to take shelter. Two days later, they covered another three miles, after which some friars hid and fed them. Four days later, Jean Baptiste and his companions shot two bulls and crafted a boat from their hides. With shoulder blades tied to sticks as paddles, the threesome miraculously sailed past a squadron of thirteen French guards undetected. Sixty miles later, they were once again on the run.[24]

Unable to locate the escapees, a furious Vaudreuil wrote to the influential minister Count de Maurepas on December 29, 1744:

> [Two Englishmen escaped]…. *This unfortunate incident also involved the man called Baureau, a settler in this colony, whom I had planned to*

send to France by the same ship, but who managed to free himself despite his being chained by his feet, hands, and neck. This man, a man with a wife and a child, had fled the colony, taking with him a girl and several slaves belonging to various individuals….

I have made every possible effort to catch this vagabond, but he has eluded me so far. This man would be especially dangerous if he went over to the side of the savages allied with our enemies because he is brave, resourceful, and well liked by all the nations of this continent.[25]

Jean Baptiste was now a man on the run—no wife, no lover and no boat. But he did have friends who had the ear of Governor Vaudreuil and beyond.

Jean Baptiste stayed on the move. He was bitter but hopeful—bitter that he had lost everything (money, land and mistress)[26] but hopeful to receive a king's pardon. Popular with various Indian nations, Jean Baptiste eluded capture for three years, earning a living however he could, including the selling of slaves.[27]

Oddly enough, the two persons Jean Baptiste had hurt the most—the wife he betrayed and stole from and the governor who put a price on his head—joined forces to secure the pardon he sought. Vaudreuil wrote to the king's minister:

With regard to the kidnapping of the girl, she entirely absolves him from blame in her depositions, claiming that it was she who encouraged him to take that action. And the negroes which this settler has been accused of stealing, have been found to be the property of his wife and his father. Furthermore, the man is busily moving about the colony and is constantly begging for a pardon by means of his wife, who claims that he is sorry for his mistakes. I thought that by putting a price on his head I would get some cooperation from the savages, but they all took the opposite position, providing him protection and constantly urging me in the strongest terms to grant him his pardon.[28]

On October 20, 1747, after three years, during which each day might be his last as a free man, a ship came from France bearing what Jean Baptiste and his allies had sought: an official pardon from King Louis XV himself. It was only a partial pardon—one that required Jean Baptiste to leave Louisiana for good and make his way to France. Once again, Governor Vaudreuil intervened on behalf of his former adversary, requesting a full pardon. He wrote glowingly of the man's remorse and recent exemplary behavior. He also warned of the esteem with which various tribes held the renegade. Maurepas relented, and Jean Baptiste was once again a free (legally) man.[29]

Jean Baptiste repaid his recent benefactors by embracing a life of dissipation. He began sleeping with loose women, gambling, squandering his money and abusing alcohol.[30] Jean Baptiste's escapades became such a scandal that his father disinherited him in 1750. Fortunately for Jean Baptiste, he still had his wife, Catherine, to fall back on. But then he messed that up too. He would show up at random times at his wife's house, often bringing with him cronies nearly as wild as he. His drunkenness became such an issue that Catherine took her and Jean Baptiste's four children to New Orleans and then filed for a bodily separation to keep her husband away from her person, children and property. Eventually, Jean Baptiste agreed to a permanent and legal separation.[31]

In September 1757, a Spanish ship sank off the coast of Cat Island. The ever-resourceful and financially desperate Jean Baptiste began to loot the sunken ship. Unfortunately for him, France and Spain were at peace, and a twelve-man French garrison (including four Swiss mercenaries) on Cat Island arrested the scavenger. Once again, Jean Baptiste sat in prison awaiting shipment to New Orleans. His profligate life since his pardon a decade before ensured that he would be facing a stiff penalty. Having alienated and embarrassed all who had stood up for him, Jean Baptiste's fate looked gloomy.

And yet, the smooth-talking renegade was able to bribe his guards into releasing him from prison. Still, he found himself on Cat Island, seven miles from the mainland and without a boat. Having convinced two Swiss soldiers to desert with him, the threesome waited until the French commander returned in the evening, and then one of the disgruntled Swiss killed him. The escapee and deserters then forced a French soldier at gunpoint into the boat (so as to leave no witnesses) and made their way to the mainland, where they planned to flee to English territory.

The new governor of New Orleans, Louis Billouart Kerlerec, immediately sent word to the commander at Mobile and to the Alabama Indians to either arrest or kill the perpetrators. It did not take long to apprehend Jean Baptiste. Not long after, the two Swiss and French deserters were captured in an English cabin. The Swiss assassin promptly fell on his sword to avoid capture. Like Jean Baptiste, the remaining Swiss and Frenchman were taken in shackles to New Orleans, where the authorities were determined that there would be no more escapes.

Jean Baptiste's luck had run out.

Torture with Sharp Points and Wheels, by Antonio Tempesta (early seventeenth century). *Rijksmuseum.*

June 7, 1757

The captured Frenchman was exonerated as a forced accomplice. The Swiss was handed over to his unit "which administered to him the most exemplary justice. He was sentenced by assembly of their council to be sawed in half, his head and a hand amputated, both of which would be displayed on a gibbet for eight days, and these things were carried out."[32]

Jean Baptiste—smuggler, scavenger, lover, brigand and convict—was sentenced to death on the wheel. The official report read:

> …*were sentenced to have their bodies broken, alive; to die upon the wheel;*
> *and to have their bodies cut into 4 pieces and thrown on the garbage dump,*
> *all of which had been carried out, in front of the troops, three hours after*
> *the sentence was handed down.*[33]

News of Jean Baptiste's barbaric death spread along the coast. Governor Kerlerec had sent a clear and ominous message to the deserters, smugglers and pirates of the Gulf Coast. Nevertheless, the majority of coastal residents were indignant at the treatment of one of their own. Kerlerec's cruelty led to his recall to France five years later, in 1762.

By then, Jean Baptiste's dismembered body lay unburied and scattered across New Orleans' city dump. But the legend of the Choctaw-French man who had defied two governors and twice escaped from prison, and who had received a pardon from the king of France himself, only to squander it by killing a royal officer and fleeing to enemy territory, would grow over the years.

And so would his progeny.

Chapter 2

THE GULF COAST DURING THE AMERICAN REVOLUTIONARY WAR, 1779–1783

THE SPANISH

1777, New Orleans
Bernardo de Galvez

In 1777, relations between Spain and Great Britain were deteriorating. It seemed that war was inevitable. Fortunately for Spanish Louisiana, a warrior had just been appointed governor.

Bernardo de Galvez was the nephew of Commander General of the Interior Provinces Jose de Galvez. His father was Mattias de Galvez, the captain general of Guatemala. No doubt family connections opened doors that otherwise would have been closed to the modestly born son of Málaga, Spain. But the Galvez name also brought with it certain expectations. Bernardo de Galvez was one of those rare leaders who justified his nepotistic patronage.

Galvez entered a hornet's nest when he first docked at New Orleans. The Crescent City had recently—much to the chagrin of the French population—been secretly ceded by France to Spain at the conclusion of the Seven Years' War. Protests, petitions and rebellions were all put down by previous Spanish governors—some of them ruthlessly.[34] The French population was in no mood to receive yet another Spanish governor. And yet Galvez would be different. He endeared himself to the local French leaders. He married a local girl—Marie Félicité de Saint-Maxent

Bernardo de Galvez. *Beinecke Library at Yale University.*

d'Estrehan—promoted trade with France and, recognizing the damage that Spanish mercantilism was doing to New Orleans, wisely turned a blind eye to smuggling. Scotsman turned Pensacola resident James Bruce wrote glowingly, and worriedly, of the new governor:

> *His name is Galvez, nephew of the Spanish minister for the Department of the Indies; he is young, gay and courteous....*[He] *enters into all their parties of pleasure and amusements and professes what really seems to be very natural to him, an evident partiality for the French nation....The gay, volatile inhabitants of Louisiana...have now got their every wish, their trade is opened, and even their very foibles countenanced by their new governor, in return for which they almost pay him adoration, in so much that in the event of a war between our Crown and theirs its generally believed that it would take thousands where hundreds only would have been necessary before his arrival* [to take New Orleans].[35]

There was no need for Galvez to endear himself to his own soldiers. He had done that years before when he displayed uncommon valor on the battlefield against the feared Apaches. In an attempt to keep the fierce and daring warriors away from the Spanish missions on the borderlands, Galvez, who at the time was stationed in present-day Mexico, led an army north. He told his men:

> *Alone I would go without having anyone to accompany me; and I will either take a scalp to Chihuahua and perform my duty or pay with my life for the king's bread that I have eaten. There is the road from our land, follow it those of you who have faint hearts; but follow me those of you who wish to take part in my glorious hardships, follow me on the assumption that I can give you nothing but thanks for this fineness, but that it will live always in my memory and recollection.*[36]

During the battles against the Apaches, Galvez was seriously wounded but continued to fight, further solidifying the loyalty of his troops:

> *Notwithstanding the fact that I was convalescing from a serious illness, and that my slight or negligible strength would have excused me from mounting a horse, as soon as the function was over and I learned that my men were after the Indians, although no soldier remained to accompany me, I set out alone to join them. It was my misfortune, however, before meeting my soldiers to encounter five Indians, who, after a long while, left me wounded, struck in the arm by an arrow and with two lance thrusts in the chest.*[37]

When Galvez returned from the borderlands to accept the governorship of Louisiana (after spending three years in Spain and Algiers as a professor and colonel), war loomed with England. Before he accepted his post on January 1, 1777, Galvez graciously and inspiringly addressed the citizens of New Orleans:

> *I cannot avail myself of my commission without previously swearing before the Cabildo, that I shall defend the province; but, although I am disposed to shed the last drop of my blood for Louisiana and for my king, I cannot take an oath which I may be exposed to violate, because I do not know if you will help me in resisting the ambitious designs of the English. What do you say? Shall I take the oath of governor? Shall I swear to defend Louisiana?*[38]

In an astonishingly brief period of time, Galvez had united a bitterly divided province. Now he could turn his full attention to the aggressions of the English over in Pensacola.

1779–1780
The Natchez-Mobile Campaign

On May 18, 1779, New Orleans governor Bernardo de Galvez received reliable word that war with Great Britain was inevitable and imminent. He immediately saw a tremendous opportunity: he would no longer have to defend a large swath of territory, nor would he have to defend New Orleans from potential attacks from a variety of directions. Instead, Galvez planned to take the fight to the British. And he would do so promptly.[39]

The Mississippi River controlled the interior of the North American continent. With the Atlantic Seaboard blockaded by His Britannic Majesty, the importance of the Mississippi River increased exponentially. Consequently, the British manned three forts with men and cannons to protect the crucial waterway: Manchac, Baton Rouge and Natchez. Galvez planned to capture all three and to do so before the British in Pensacola got word of the declaration of war. If he was to pull off this improbable coup, Galvez needed absolute secrecy. Thus, he continued to communicate with his British counterpart, John Campbell in Pensacola. He even kept his germinating plan from his own council and soldiers.

Galvez planned to put his ambitious plan into action on August 22. It consisted of nothing less than capturing *all* British forts south of Memphis and along the Gulf Coast, including Pensacola—the largest harbor in the northern Gulf. His council was aghast and strongly recommended that he take a different course of action. Galvez refused and prepared to march his army north to British Manchac.

And then disaster struck. On August 18, four days before his campaign was to begin, a hurricane ravaged the town of New Orleans. Galvez would later report:

> [A] *violent hurricane arrived and in less than three hours sank all of the ships…among them the small warships and gunboats I had ordered to be built for the defense of the river. Many houses in the city and most of those around it were also destroyed, supplies lost, trees torn, men dismayed, their women and children wandering through the deserted fields*

Map of Louisiana (1775). *Beinecke Library at Yale University.*

*abandoned to the elements, the lands flooded, and everything drowned in
the river, along with my resources, supplies, and hopes.*[40]

A lesser man would have been discouraged by this "act of God." But
Galvez was made of stronger stuff.

September 1779
The Mississippi River Campaign

Although Galvez is most remembered for his capture of Pensacola, his
battles along the Mississippi River turned the course of the war.

Although it was a tactically impressive campaign, Galvez's true genius lay
in his strategic vision. Hindsight confirms his brilliance. While he certainly
expected a British attack at some point, somewhere, Galvez could not have
known that this attack was imminent, for the British had already planned to

seize a poorly guarded New Orleans. General Campbell in Pensacola had received orders to take the Crescent City in conjunction with another British force headed down the Mississippi River from Canada.[41]

But Galvez was one step ahead of his adversary. He wrote to the Captain General in Havana:

> *I believe that you will not disapprove my resolution to attack them first, taking advantage of their ignorance of the declaration of war; for if this opportunity had been allowed to pass, and they had had time to put their plans into execution, there is no doubt there would have been a very different outcome for our arms in this province.*[42]

Galvez's first target was Fort Bute in British-occupied Manchac. It would be the easiest, as it was guarded by only twenty-seven soldiers. (Fearing an *American* attack, British lieutenant colonel Alexander Dickson had taken the bulk of his own army north toward Baton Rouge.) Having already lost a third of his force on the difficult and swampy eleven-mile march, Galvez wasted no time taking the fort. Because he was determined to keep his mission a secret from the British, he also kept it from his men. On the night of September 6, he finally announced to his army that war had been declared between Spain and Britain and that they were to commence hostilities by taking Manchac. The Spaniards and Indian allies stormed the fort in the morning, killed one Briton and captured twenty. (Six British escaped north to warn Baton Rouge that Galvez was on his way with about one thousand troops.)[43]

The fort at Baton Rouge proved much more difficult. The British had 550 men, including 400 regulars, and thirteen cannon behind a ditch eighteen feet wide and nine feet deep. Inside stood an earthen wall surrounded by a *chevaux de frise*, a barrier of sharp wooden spikes. Galvez's enthusiastic officers—perhaps buoyed by the easy victory at Manchac, perhaps fearing dwindling supplies and the inevitable summer fevers—urged a direct assault on the fort. Galvez demurred, declaring:

> *Most of my small army was composed of inhabitants; and that any setback would cover the colony with mourning....I do all that is possible to conserve the lives of Militia men who are fathers of families which comprise half of the colony. In these we have the hope of an enlarged, future force.*[44]

Instead of an assault, Galvez ordered his men to prepare for a bombardment. However, a siege could take up to two months. Certainly by then either a British relief force would be on its way to Baton Rouge, or, more dangerously, an expedition would be on its way to take New Orleans. Thus, Galvez could risk neither a frontal assault nor a protracted siege. In addition, he had only ten cannons to the British thirteen. To negate those poor odds, he would rely on trickery.

There was a clump of trees near one side of the fort that provided obvious protection to a besieging army. Galvez ordered a large number of his men to the grove with orders to be noisy. Some chopped down trees, some dug ditches and still others fired on the British fort from the cover of trees, as if they were protecting a unit of sappers and miners. The British, in turn, directed most of their cannons at the wooded Spaniards.

Meantime, Galvez's most reliable soldiers were digging a trench on the other side of the fort, behind a small fence. When complete, they moved their own cannons into the fresh trenches and mounted them on wooden platforms.

When day came, the British realized their costly mistake. The Spaniards began firing away with their cannons from musket-shot range. Several hours later, Colonel Dickson raised the white flag. Galvez accepted his surrender on the condition that Dickson also surrender Fort Panmure in Natchez. Realizing that Natchez, with only eighty soldiers, could not defend itself against Galvez, Dickson acquiesced. Galvez sent one of his captains to receive Natchez's surrender, which occurred on October 5. (A few days after surrendering to Galvez, the Natchez commander received word from General Campbell in Pensacola that war had been declared and to prepare to invade New Orleans.) Spain was now in possession of the forts at Manchac, Baton Rouge and Natchez.

During his five-week Mississippi campaign, Galvez lost one man killed and two wounded (not counting those who died or fell ill due to disease). In exchange, he captured more than one thousand enemy regulars and militia, three forts, eight ships and 1,300 miles of Mississippi River farmland.[45]

The Mississippi River campaign was only the beginning of Galvez's coastal ambitions.

January–March 1780
Mobile

While the Spanish authorities were pleased with Galvez's Mississippi campaign, the real objective remained the conquest of the Gulf Coast. Galvez had received a royal order:

Fort Conde, Mobile, Alabama, by Carol Highsmith (2010). *Library of Congress.*

The king has determined that the principal object of his forces in America during the war against the English shall be to expel them from the Gulf of Mexico and the banks of the Mississippi where their establishments are so prejudicial to our commerce and also to the security of our more valuable possessions.[46]

On January 11, 1780, Galvez set sail for Mobile with 754 men. Despite terrible storms that wreaked havoc on his ships, Galvez's expedition finally landed at the doorstep of Fort Charlotte and immediately commenced to lay siege to the British fort.[47]

Captain Elias Durnford had heard that seven hundred Spaniards died at sea during the storm. He soon learned that this was wishful thinking. Now his goal was to hold out as long as possible until reinforcements arrived from Pensacola. Unfortunately for him, the note from General John Campbell explaining that relief was, in fact, on its way was intercepted by Galvez.

While the captured note left Durnford in the dark, it greatly disturbed Galvez. In front stood a stubborn garrison led by a brave commander. Thirty miles away, to the east, was a relief force of roughly six hundred soldiers. Galvez sent out pickets to keep his army from being surprised and then urgently ordered his cannons to pound Fort Charlotte into quick submission.

Meanwhile, on March 10, Campbell was building enough rafts to carry his men down the Mobile River to Fort Charlotte. As they made their final preparations, Campbell noticed an eerie silence. The cannons thirty miles distant had all gone silent.

Captain Durnford, unaware of Campbell's approach and not willing to endanger the inhabitants of Mobile any more than necessary, raised the white flag. He asked Galvez that his soldiers be allowed to withdraw to Pensacola. Galvez promptly denied that request, but he did allow the Britons to surrender with full military honors. And then he added the following ominous provision: those citizens who had taken arms against him would also be considered prisoners of war. If, however, Galvez did not attack Pensacola within eight months, the citizen-soldiers would all be released on parole. There was now no doubt that Pensacola was Galvez's ultimate goal.

Immediately after taking Fort Charlotte, Galvez began repairing its breaches and weak points. After all, Campbell was still only one hard day's march away—or so Galvez thought. Unbeknownst to him, Campbell had already begun the long march back to Pensacola.[48]

The capture of Mobile, as well as Galvez's conduct throughout the brief siege, permanently disrupted the balance of power on the Gulf Coast.

Indian tribes, especially the Creeks and Choctaws, were beginning to question their allegiance to Great Britain, which had now lost four forts and more than half of West Florida's land to Galvez's troops. In addition, the gumbo pot of races along the same coast were also questioning their allegiances. Britain had presented itself as an economic powerhouse and the defender of liberty. And yet here was Bernardo de Galvez, pawn of the Catholic king of Spain, despot and tyrant, behaving with the utmost chivalry and offering generous terms to both surrendering soldiers and the colonists now living under his authority.

Even the Indians loyal to Britain began to doubt the wisdom of allying with King George to fight the Spaniards. After all, could not the Spanish provide similar trade opportunities and offer equivalent gifts? These questions and the Indian response would have significant consequences one year later at Pensacola.

THE RENEGADES

1781, Pensacola
William Augustus Bowles

The Spanish began what had become the routine shelling of British-held Queen's Redoubt.[49] As long as His Majesty's troops held this outpost, there was hope that Pensacola could be saved. Any day now—or so the garrison hoped—a relief force would arrive. Any day, the sails of His Britannic Majesty's ships would appear in the harbor. Until then, the Spaniards unleashed a barrage, day after day, at the hapless fort.

One of the fort's defenders was seventeen-year-old William Augustus Bowles. Reared in a staunchly Loyalist family, Bowles left home at thirteen to enlist in the British army. After serving in Philadelphia and New York, the young ensign[50] was sent south to Jamaica. After rough winds separated his transport from its convoy and disease ravaged his unit, killing his captain and regimental surgeon, the remainder of Bowles's detachment was assigned to help defend Pensacola against the increasingly active Bernardo de Galvez.

Never one to mince words or to defer to another, Bowles had a falling out with one of his commanders at Pensacola and fled the garrison in the company of some Lower Creeks who had come seeking gifts. For the next two years, he lived among the Muskogees,[51] eventually intermarrying and

William Augustus Bowles, by Thomas Hardy (1791). *National Portrait Gallery.*

having children.[52] When it became clear that Pensacola would, in fact, be attacked by Spain, he went to do his duty and fight the enemies of his king.

At first, Bowles was an exemplary soldier. When General John Campbell attempted to thwart Galvez's attack on Pensacola by recapturing Mobile,

Bowles marched at the head of a band of Creeks fifty miles from Fort George in Pensacola to Mobile and surprised the Spanish at a post just east of Mobile. Then things went downhill. The startled and outnumbered Spanish fought back and drove the British back to Pensacola. Bowles, however, distinguished himself and was one of the last to leave the battlefield, retreating only when a cannonball shattered the tree behind which he was firing. Scalps in hand, Bowles fled with the rest to Pensacola.[53]

Bowles was welcomed back into His Majesty's service and given back his rank of ensign. Glad to be among his former comrades—but still pleased that so many of his new Creek friends remained encamped outside the walls—Bowles decided to stay and defend the fort. It proved to be an ill-fated decision. Even more unfortunate, he was assigned to the trenches of Queen's Redoubt, where he was on his way to join his companions at breakfast at 9:00 a.m. on May 8.

An explosion rocked the entire redoubt, killing many instantly, burning many more and forcing the remainder to flee, as best they could, to the Prince of Wales Redoubt.[54]

The Siege of Pensacola was effectively over. The career of William Augustus Bowles, however, was just beginning.

The Spanish

March 1780-March 1781, Pensacola
Bernardo de Galvez

One year after the surrender of Mobile, British Pensacola was still under a de facto siege. Although there were no Spanish ships blockading the harbor, the residents of Pensacola understood that this could change at any moment. Their nemesis, Galvez, had time after time proven himself to be daring (sometimes recklessly so) and ambitious. Surely the descendant of conquistadors had his sights set on another target. With Galvez's troops sixty miles away in Mobile and a major Spanish fleet less than six hundred miles away in Cuba, Pensacolans understood their peril, especially the merchants, who feared that the dreaded fleet would arrive at a moment's notice, taking their ships along the way or taking them as they unloaded their wares. Consequently, the port was running perilously low on provisions.

"A Perspective View of Pensacola" (1775). *New York Public Library.*

But then hope began to pervade the colony when three hurricanes ravaged the Caribbean. Slowly, word began to spread that Galvez was dead, swept into oblivion by the deadly winds. (Three successive hurricanes on October 3, 10 and 18, 1780, devastated the islands of the Caribbean Sea. The winds of the hurricane on the tenth exceeded two hundred miles per hour and killed more than twenty-two thousand people—the deadliest hurricane in history. Galvez himself was sailing from Cuba to Pensacola when his fleet was ravaged by the October 18 hurricane, which scattered his fleet and killed hundreds of sailors, forcing him to return to Cuba and delay his masterstroke by half a year.)[55] Confidence gradually seeped back into the community, and a ship docked in the harbor decided that with the Spanish threat likely neutralized, it was now time to make a run. Eager Pensacolans began placing orders for London goods. Sugar, tea, coffee, wine, rum, clothes and furniture would soon make their way to Pensacola once again. The town grew cautiously optimistic by the day.[56]

But then March 9, 1781, arrived. Cannons began to explode south of the town. The Spanish had arrived.

BRITISH COMMANDER JOHN CAMPBELL was not confident of his prospects. He doubted how much Britain cared about Pensacola. After all, His Majesty was fighting a world war on seemingly endless fronts. Not only was he trying to put down the uprising in the thirteen rebelling colonies, but he was also trying to make sure that Canada did not become the fourteenth to rebel.

(The Continental Congress had been dreaming and scheming to take the northern colony from Britain from the beginning and had already made several abortive attempts to do so.) The Spanish and French had laid siege to British Gibraltar two years earlier. St. Augustine, the capital of East Florida, was in danger and begging for reinforcements. Lord Charles Cornwallis's southern army needed more and more men as it marched north in an attempt to finally destroy General Nathanael Greene and separate the southern colonies from the rest of the rebellion. And then there was the Caribbean.

Thirteen colonies joined the rebellion against Great Britain. Seventeen remained loyal. While the North American mainland colonies were the largest (the thirteen rebel colonies plus Canada and the two Floridas), the Caribbean colonies were far and away the most profitable. Just one of those West Indian colonies, Jamaica, brought in almost as much revenue as the rebellious colonies combined.[57] Add in a handful of other islands (and India as well) and Britain had its hands full, trying to keep the contagion of independence from spreading and protect the valuable sugar lands from foreign invasion—especially after Spain and France joined the war with their powerful fleets in 1778 and 1779.[58]

Simply put, Pensacola was not a priority for a nation fighting a war around the globe with increasingly limited resources. General Campbell understood this. Nevertheless, he immediately dispatched a ship to Jamaica begging for reinforcements. More realistically, he sought aid from his Indian allies to the north, specifically the Creeks and Choctaws.

Only a fraction of the expected Indian allies arrived to defend Pensacola, roughly five hundred warriors, most of whom were Choctaw. (The British had been skimping on gifts the last few years and now paid the price for it. In addition, there had recently been several false alarms in which warriors showed up to fight the Spanish only to find no imminent threat. They then walked several hundred miles back to their villages.) To many Indian allies, the stingy Campbell had cried "wolf" one too many times.

Meanwhile, Galvez landed his troops on Santa Rosa Island, opposite Pensacola, without any opposition. He hoped to sail around the British Royal Navy Redoubt, but his naval officers were frightened of the battery's cannons and knew the British guns to be too high for Spanish cannons to retaliate; they feared that the ships would be sitting ducks. Instead, the captains insisted on a landing left of the fort.

Racing against a potential British relief force, as well as dwindling food supplies, Galvez needed to move on Pensacola itself. He was convinced that

Spanish ships could run the gauntlet beneath the battery. The redoubt was high up on the red bluffs—perhaps too high. Galvez gambled that if he hugged the shoreline just north of Santa Rosa Island, the British batteries wouldn't have the accuracy to hit him.

March 18, 1781
Pensacola Bay, Beneath the British Royal Navy Redoubt

Galvez boarded his brigantine to the sound of a fifteen-gun salute. He wanted the timid captains behind him, his soldiers beached on Santa Rosa Island and the British gunners above to know exactly who was on deck.

Earlier that day, he had sent his captains a message: "Whoever had honor and valor would follow him, for he was going in advance with the *Galveztown* to remove fear."[59] The captain of the Spanish fleet was incensed at Galvez's insult and promised to avenge himself and the entire navy on the "audacious and unmannerly upstart, a traitor to his king and country." He would personally report Galvez's actions to the king and hoped to see Galvez hanging from his yardarm.[60]

The "audacious upstart" proceeded to run the gauntlet, to the cheers of his soldiers and the consternation of the British gunners, who fired dozens of ineffectual cannonballs at the *Galveztown*. Galvez had forced the passage. He then summoned the captain in charge of the remainder of the fleet, but he refused to follow. However, the next day, his fellow naval officers urged him to enter the bay. The Spanish fleet sailed by the cannons with not a single injury.

The lid to the coffin of British Pensacola was about to be nailed shut.

The Rest of the Siege
March 19, 1781–May 8, 1781 [61]

While Campbell for the most part remained behind his fortifications, his Indian allies, along with one hundred soldiers from Fort George, conducted guerrilla warfare against the beached Spaniards, hoping to forestall the inevitable. Spanish reinforcements began to arrive by land from Mobile; they were harassed as soon as they reached the Perdido River. The Indians also attacked any foragers or stray soldiers and sailors they found. One day, a boat carrying eleven Spanish sailors beached at the Perdido shoreline in search of forage. Ten of them were killed, and the eleventh was marched back to Pensacola, where General Campbell sent the hapless soldier off for interrogation.[62]

The Creeks and Choctaws might have saved Pensacola had there been a concerted effort by Britain to relieve the besieged city, for their constant harassment of Spanish troops and reinforcements began to take a toll, psychologically and in casualties. Their strategy was to fight, run and fight again, rarely risking their own lives. As one Upper Creek explained to a Spanish officer, "[Creeks were] frugal with the blood of their compatriots, for the reason that the nations consist of a small number of individuals.… [I]n the world there were three races of men: white, black, and red; that the first and second were innumerable, and therefore the loss of some of them was not a cause for grief; but that there were very few of the third, and therefore it was necessary to preserve them with great care."[63] The guerrilla-style fighting kept the Spanish always thinking, always worrying, always fearful. Death could come any moment from any direction. True, only a small number of Spaniards were killed during the approach to Pensacola, but the terror of instant death—or worse, capture—led to many a sleepless night for the besiegers.

As effective as the Indians were at delaying reinforcements from Mobile (of whom more than 900 did arrive in Pensacola on March 22), there was simply no way they could impede the reinforcements arriving from New Orleans via boat. On March 23, 1,400 soldiers arrived to supplement Galvez's already numerically superior army.[64]

General Campbell could read the writing on the wall. Intending to hold out as long as possible and hoping to receive miracle reinforcements (and as a humanitarian gesture to the town he had sworn to defend), Campbell withdrew his troops from Pensacola and concentrated them in Fort George, north of town. But before he did so, he wrote a letter to Galvez asking that the town and its innocent inhabitants be spared the atrocities concomitant with a siege. Although he would have been justified in shelling the town—at least by contemporary military convention—Galvez agreed to spare Pensacola itself if Campbell removed all British troops from the town. Campbell promptly complied.[65]

The vise was closing, but Galvez still had a daunting task ahead of him. Fort George was protected by two redoubts, the Prince of Wales Redoubt about 350 yards to the north and the larger Queen's Redoubt, another 350 yards north. The two fortifications were designed to protect Fort George from a land attack to the north. Both were adequately armed with soldiers and cannons, presenting a daunting and deadly task to any bold enough to storm the redoubts. Galvez decided to focus on taking Queen's Redoubt, the higher of the two. Success would enable him to turn the cannons on the two remaining British fortifications below. He ordered his men to begin digging zigzagging parallels closer and closer to Queen's Redoubt.

So, day after day, week after week, the Spanish inched closer to Fort George. Each time the soldiers moved camp, they experienced a foreshadowing of hell: fear, hard labor, surprise attacks and rain. With victory in sight, the siege became exceedingly tedious. During one of many Indian raids, Galvez was shot in the finger, and the bullet ricocheted off and struck his abdomen. The general was taken to a field hospital, where doctors feared for his life. True to his nature, Galvez quickly recovered and was back in the thick of battle.

One week after being wounded, Galvez learned that a Spanish fleet carrying more than two thousand reinforcements, including seven hundred

Fort George, Pensacola. *Collection of Ryan Starrett.*

Prise de Pensacola, by Nicolas Ponce (1784). *Library of Congress.*

French soldiers and more than enough supplies to take Fort George, arrived in Pensacola Bay. Now with seven thousand men under his command and a fleet of fifteen warships in the harbor, the fall of Fort George was all but inevitable.

Still, General Campbell would not concede. On May 4, one hundred British and eighty German allies snuck out of their trench and crept to the woods closest to the most advanced Spanish trench. While the Spaniards ate, the British unleashed a tremendous bombardment. Confident in their sturdy fortification, the Spanish soldiers continued their midday meal under the broiling sun. Unbeknownst to them, the British cannons were firing blanks so as not to harm their own men, who were now creeping up to the trench. The Brits and Germans leaped into the trench and killed forty of the stunned Spaniards, forcing the rest to flee. Campbell's men spiked the cannons and ran back to the safety of their redoubt, carrying what booty they could.[66]

Galvez was furious and ordered the trench immediately retaken. It was, and another parallel trench brought the Spanish to within two hundred yards of Queen's Redoubt. On May 8, a Spanish shell landed in the redoubt's powder magazine, causing a tremendous explosion and killing nearly one

Statue of Bernardo de Galvez, Pensacola, Florida. *Collection of Ryan Starrett.*

hundred soldiers. One of the fortunate survivors, William Augustus Bowles, was just entering the redoubt when the shell exploded. Bowles wrote that he saw "the melancholy spectacle of near a hundred men blown into the air." Bowles survived the explosion, the siege and the remainder of the war and became a thorn in the side of Spain (and Great Britain, the United States and much of the Creek Nation) for the next twenty-two years.

With Galvez now in command of the sea and the high ground, General Campbell finally acknowledged the hopelessness of his situation. He raised the white flag. Two days later, on May 10, Pensacola—and West Florida—officially became a Spanish colony.

The capture of Pensacola hastened the end of the American Revolutionary War. The siege also hastened the end of the Creeks' presence in their ancestral lands. The year 1781 was only a generation removed from 1813, when Andrew Jackson and company would decisively defeat the Red Stick Creeks (the war faction) and, seventeen years later, sign the Indian Removal Act of 1830, which sent most of the surviving Creek to Indian Territory, west of the Mississippi River.

In 2014, Galvez was granted honorary U.S. citizenship—one of only eight foreigners to be so recognized. Four years later, a large statue of the Spanish hero was unveiled at the intersection of Palafox and Wright Streets in downtown Pensacola.

Most importantly to Galvez, the king of Spain honored him with the following message: "[T]o perpetuate for posterity the memory of the heroic action in which you alone forced the entrance of the bay, you may place as the crest on your coat of arms the brig *Galveztown* with the motto 'Yo Solo.'"[67]

Chapter 3

SAN DOMINGUE AND
THE AFRICAN INFLUENCE, 1791

THE BLACKS

1791, August 14, Bois Caiman, San Domingue

The massive slave, overseer and voodoo priest Dutty Boukman calmly looked out at his people. He was ready. So were his followers. On the night of August 14, 1791, roughly two hundred slaves—mostly overseers with access to weapons and the trust of their masters—gathered at Bois Caiman (Alligator Woods). The conspirators were about to embark on a dangerous, bloody and deadly mission. Boukman needed to reassure his army that God was on their side.

> *The god who created the sun which gives us light, who rouses the waves and rules the storm, though hidden in the clouds, he watches us. He sees all the white man does.*
>
> *The god of the white man inspires him with crime, but our god calls upon us to do good works. Our god who is good to us orders us to revenge our wrongs. He will direct our arms and aid us. Throw away the symbol of the god of the whites who has so often caused us to weep, and listen to the voice of liberty, which speaks in the hearts of us all.*[68]

Frenchman Antoine Dalmas wrote a contemporary account of the historical moment in which he displays the French planters' contempt for their slaves:

> *Before executing their plan, they celebrated a kind of fete or sacrifice, in the middle of a wooded, uncultivated ground on the Choiseul plantation, called* Caiman [Alligator], *where the Negroes assembled in very great number. A completely black pig, surrounded with fetishes, loaded down with offerings, each more bizarre than the other, was the holocaust offered to the all-powerful genie of the black race. The religious ceremonies that the negroes practiced in cutting the pig's throat, the eagerness with which they drank the pig's blood, and their desire for the prize that each one wanted to possess, a kind of talisman, that, according to them, would render them invulnerable, all serve to characterize the African.*[69]

Like Dalmas, the Europeans of San Domingue and its neighboring islands expected the rebellion to peter out as quickly as it started. It was led, after all, by primitive Africans, surely incapable of any organized mass resistance. And yet, within eight days, Boukman's army had burned two hundred plantations. Within six weeks, he had an army numbering between twenty thousand and eighty thousand soldiers. This was no isolated slave rebellion but a full-blown war.[70] Historian Carolyn Fick explained the methodical nature of the slaves' objectives: "[Boukman's soldiers] took to destroy…not only the cane fields, but also the manufacturing installations, sugar mills, tools and other farm equipment, storage bins, and slave quarters; in short, every material manifestation of their existence under slavery and its means of exploitation."[71] A local French planter marveled, "There is a motor that powers them and keeps powering them and that we cannot come to know."[72]

Boukman's ceremony on that stormy night in Bois Caiman was the birth of Haiti. He and his followers—and those who carried the fight on after their founder's death—would establish the Western Hemisphere's first Black republic. The fact that they did so amid a White imperialist world and on the most prosperous of the sugar islands is a testament to the slaves' solidarity and determination.

But first there would be a dozen years of brutal fighting, with atrocities committed by each side, casting war in its worst light. White owners retaliated and killed thousands of enslaved. Slaves paid back atrocity for atrocity—and then turned on each other. Boukman himself was killed three months after

Toussaint Louverture, leader of the Haitian revolution. *New York Public Library.*

he raised the standard of rebellion, and his head was placed atop a pike in the central plaza of Cap Français as a warning to the rebelling slaves.

The warning went unheeded. By 1803, new Haitian leaders—Henry Christophe, Jean-Jacques Dessalines and Toussaint Louverture, all inspired by Boukman—had liberated San Domingue from European colonialism and slavery.

NOT ALL OF SAN Domingue's residents welcomed emancipation. The plantation owners who had turned the island into the world's most profitable colony on the backs of Africans had the most to lose. But so did their mixed children and the free persons of color. The latter—often a result of being the former—had filled the necessary middle-class void left by planters who wanted little, if anything, to do with industry and craftsmanship. In many instances, the free persons of color who had embraced the roles of blacksmith, tailor, stonecutter and various artisans had advanced beyond many of the island's Whites, at least economically. Now they had a stake in their world, and when that world was turned upside down, many free persons of color joined the emigration from San Domingue.

Of the twenty-five thousand refugees who fled to the United States during the Haitian Revolution, fifteen thousand ended up in New Orleans. In 1810 alone, ten thousand immigrants arrived, doubling the Crescent City's population.[73] The sudden influx of so many migrants changed New Orleans in three ways: it reaffirmed the predominance of French culture, further loosened the sexual mores between the races and led to much stricter laws regulating slavery.

THE ARRIVAL OF THOUSANDS of San Domingue planters and merchants coincided with the United States' takeover in 1803. At the same time many, Americans—"Kaintucks"—began pouring into the city in search of economic opportunity. Naturally, the competition for economic and cultural dominance commenced—Americans versus Francophiles. A stroll through New Orleans in 1803, 1814 or 2022 would provide the ambler with concrete evidence of the cultural victor. New Orleans has always been and continues to be more Caribbean than American. At the turn of the nineteenth century, just as the Americans were beginning to challenge French hegemony, the arrival of so many planters and artisans from San Domingue (and their more than four thousand slaves) was considered a great boon by most in New Orleans.

While the city was on its way to becoming an economic powerhouse, the San Domingue émigrés added flair and culture to the "northern most Caribbean city." Historian Lyle Saxon wrote of the new immigrants:

> This was a highly civilized, somewhat decadent, brilliant group of men and women; and they brought with them their civilization, their charm, their intelligence—and their vices. Some of them opened schools, some taught dancing or music; a troupe of comedians from Cape Francoise opened a theater in New Orleans. The city became gayer and more frivolous than before. Among this group were some famous men, and many of the emigres were titled personages. They soon formed a sort of society of their own and exerted an influence in the social life of the city.[74]

Francophiles, who had bemoaned the French transfer of New Orleans to Spain and the subsequent reannexing, only to then be sold to the Americans, were delighted that so many fellow Frenchmen were arriving. It seemed that New Orleans was destined to fall into the economic and legal orbit of the United States, but its leading citizens were determined to preserve their French culture.

The arrival of the San Domingue refugees further normalized White-Black sexual relations. Although already a relatively tolerant city in terms of sexual mores (wives initially came to the early French colonists from the Salpetriere, a prison for prostitutes in Paris), the White San Domingue émigrés brought with them an even more tolerant view of interracial relationships.

Back on the island, "mulatto" mistresses could be found in every community. C.L.R. James wrote of the "dance-halls, and private brothels whereby the Mulatto women lived in such comfort and luxury that in 1789, of 7,000 Mulatto women in San Domingo, 5,000 were either prostitutes or the kept mistresses of white men."[75] The custom of kept women continued on arrival in the Crescent City, and a ritualized system of *plaçage* was de facto codified. A White man would arrange a relationship with a free woman of color in which he would feed and house her. The woman would make the best match she could and return the social and material benefits with sexual favors. The man could visit and stay at her cottage as long as he pleased. When he married—always a White woman—the *plaçage* arrangement would continue if he so chose. Should he end the relationship, the cottage remained with the *placee*.

Landing a White benefactor was a woman's assertion of her own agency, the way by which she had a say in her future and a way to ensure a livelihood for her and her children. (Children of *plaçage* benefited from social and economic connections to the father/patron.)

White-Black sexual relations—almost always a White man in a position of authority and a subservient Black or mixed woman—were common in eighteenth- and nineteenth-century America. However, in most places, it was an embarrassing and ill-kept secret to have mixed-race children wandering around the plantation and vicinity. Everyone knew where they came from. In New Orleans, such caramel skin was accepted; it was the norm, not merely tolerated but encouraged through the system of *plaçage*. Lyle Saxon wrote in his usual colorful way:

> [T]*hese were the young ladies who went out in society, who were chaperoned within an inch of their lives, and who made good marriages when they*

A French Creole, by M.J. Burns (1887). *New York Public Library.*

could. We never hear of the "innocence of young Southern manhood." And from the stories repeated sometimes by old gentlemen, it is safe to say that our great grandfathers had a good time.[76]

Author Isabel Allende, in her moving novel *Island Beneath the Sea*, wrote of the beauty of this ever-growing mixed race:

The whites had succeeded in passing a law that forbade women of color to wear a hat, jewels, or showy clothes in public places, under threat of a lashing. The result was that the mulattas adorned themselves in their tignons with such charm that they surpassed the finest hat from Paris, and displayed necklines so tempting that any jewel would have been a distraction; they had such elegant bearing that by comparison the white women looked like washerwomen.[77]

For several generations, the system of *plaçage* benefited the young, White bon vivants of New Orleans. It benefited the increasingly lighter-skinned mulatto women who would otherwise be forced to live as slaves or unkept prostitutes. *Plaçage* benefited everyone—except the fastest-growing segments of the population: slaves and free persons of color.

The inevitable result of *plaçage* was a growing population of free persons of color who, like they did in San Domingue, began to fill the role of craftsmen and artisans (and *placees*). And yet, like in San Domingue, a free person of color was a person apart. They lived a chameleon existence between two worlds. They were not slaves, had legally protected rights and possessed what the enslaved could only dream of: security, especially when it came to family. On the other hand, free persons of color could not vote, were at the whim of White-enacted laws and were denied entry into the upper echelons of society. They were free but not equal. As one of the characters in Anne Rice's masterful novel about the New Orleans *gens de couleur* explains:

We are a doomed people.... There's no equality. And there never will be. Our only hope is to hold on to our land here, to buy and to cultivate more land so that we can keep our community as a world apart. Because the white Anglo-Saxon heart is so hardened against us that there's no hope for our descendants as the Anglo-Saxon takes over, as he supplants the French and the Spanish families around us who understood us and respected us. No, there is only one hope and that is for our descendants to pass when they can into the white race. And with each one who passes, we are diminished,

Haitian revolutionaries taking revenge on French soldiers, published in 1805. *Library of Congress.*

our world and our class dies. That's what we are, Marcel, a dying people, if we are a people at all, flowers of the French and the Spanish and the African, and the Americans have put a boot to our face.[78]

Fully one-third of Black people in New Orleans were free persons of color in 1803.[79]

The lasting effect of the Haitian Revolution was fear. The White émigrés brought with them horrible and ghastly stories of what they endured on the island. (Likewise, Black slaves brought with them terrifying and brutal stories of life on the sugar plantations, where masters exerted little effort to keep their labor force alive, for it was cheaper to work a slave to death in six or seven years and then buy another—they simply imported more slaves.)

Slave owners historically have feared revolt. That fear was magnified in the American South and, in particular, the Deep South, where slaves equaled or outnumbered their masters—just as they had done at San Domingue. Failed Maroon colonies and slave rebellions in the swamps south of New Orleans in 1783 and at Point Coupee in 1795 had the White population on edge. After word reached New Orleans of the Haitian revolt and the slaves' subsequent defeat of one colonial superpower after another, including Napoleon Bonaparte, Whites across the city began to prepare for the worst. Exaggerated tales of African debauchery spread through the French Quarter and beyond. White heads were being severed and placed on pikes along the highway (just as twenty-three Black heads were displayed after Point Coupee). Babies were being systematically slaughtered. White women were being ravished.

Louisiana passed a law forbidding Caribbean Blacks from being imported into the state (the implication being that Louisiana Blacks were satisfied with their lot, with no thought of revolting against their paternalistic masters). A checkpoint was established south of the city to keep "the cannibals of the terrible republic"[80] from landing and inciting another bloodthirsty rebellion. Even President Jefferson weighed in, cautioning, "If this combustion can be introduced among us under any veil whatsoever…we have to fear it."[81]

On the night of January 8, 1811, Jefferson's words became prophetic. The slaves of Louisiana's German Coast arose, "cr[ied] havoc and let slip the dogs of war."[82]

Chapter 4

WILLIAM AUGUSTUS BOWLES AND THE STATE OF MUSKOGEE, 1792–1803

THE RENEGADES

1792–1798, West Florida
William Augustus Bowles

St. Mark's, West Florida

The Spanish government was faced with a conundrum in devising a policy toward its new northern neighbor. Historically speaking, republics tended to be weak and short-lived. It was widely believed in many European circles that the United States would not survive. Certainly, it would not pose a significant threat to the colonial powers of Great Britain, France and Spain in the long term. Rather, surely, the North American continent was up for grabs—and would presumably be divvied up between France, Great Britain and Spain.

In the meantime, Spain needed a clear policy toward these upstart states. Said policy was complicated by native tribes and confederations, namely the powerful Creeks. Spain, like its two colonial rivals, preferred to buy the allegiance of the tribes that could potentially do it the most harm. For Spain, that meant the Creeks. In exchange for allegiance to the king of Spain, the Creeks would receive much-needed trade goods, particularly muskets, balls and powder.

In addition to allies in the event of war, Spain hoped to establish a powerful buffer between its colonies and its new northern neighbors. Although Spain had fought on the same side as the United States against Great Britain just a generation before, the two were never allies. In fact, there had been tension between the two all along, as the thirteen colonies had initially hoped to be sixteen, with Canada, East Florida and West Florida joining the fight. When Bernardo de Galvez took Pensacola in 1781, Americans rejoiced. However, the spirit of cooperation was to be short-lived.[83]

Attempting to weaken the fledgling but aggressive United States, Spain began to encourage the western U.S. states to secede and form their own government—preferably under Spain, but an independent nation would work just as well. Additionally, Spain decided to arm the Creeks as a buffer to U.S. encroachment. Unfortunately, Spain did not possess the ability to effectively equip its potential allies. However, a recent Spanish resident readily proposed a tempting offer.

Scottish-born William Panton fled Savannah to St. Augustine when American forces confiscated his property after the Revolutionary War. When St. Augustine was ceded to Spain shortly after, Panton decided to stay put. He promised his new government that he would provide the necessary materiel to the Creeks, in exchange for a monopoly. A deal was struck. Panton would establish warehouses from which he would sell his goods to Indians, and in exchange, Spain would patrol the Gulf and eliminate any illegal trade. In the meantime, the recently armed Creeks would help protect the Spanish hinterlands from the United States.[84]

Panton and his partners, John Leslie and John Forbes, established one of their warehouses six miles above St. Marks, Florida, just two hundred land miles from the motherhouse in Pensacola. The reach of Panton, Leslie & Company was massive, and the partners soon became exceedingly wealthy. In 1784, one of the most powerful of the Creek chiefs, Alexander McGillivray, joined the firm as a silent partner.[85]

Creek hunters began to exchange deerskins and other goods at Panton's store for muskets and bullets. Soon, the deer population began to diminish considerably, but Panton's prices stayed the same or rose. The Creeks found themselves deeper and deeper in debt. The solution, all too often, was to sell land to the United States to pay off Panton.

William Augustus Bowles—once again living among the Creeks after the surrender of Pensacola to Galvez—saw the danger of dealing with Panton. He asked that Spain instead work through him to arm the Creeks. When Spain declined, Bowles began to entreat Great Britain. He campaigned for free trade. In particular, he promised the merchants of Nassau that once he took control of Muskogee (Bowles's name for the new Creek state he hoped to found), he would begin ship construction, and within six months, his ships would be bringing raw materials into British West Indian ports. In short, Muskogee would be able to supply the various islands with desperately needed essentials, such as timber, as well as valuable trade goods, like deerskin.[86]

With Britain onboard (or Spain, or an independent Muskogee state), Bowles would serve (lead) the Creeks by opening two ports on the Indian River and Apalachee River. He would sell them British materiel at a much lower cost than Panton. The Creeks would no longer need to sell their land to the Americans to pay off an exorbitant Panton. Most Creeks were growing tired of dealing with Panton, but they doubted Bowles's ability to deliver on his extravagant promises. Bowles needed to prove his mettle—to the British authorities, certainly, but mostly to his Creek constituents.

THERE WAS A PRICE on Bowles's head. His influence was waning. He had been unable to procure the materiel and trade goods he had promised. It was time to make a bold move. It was time to cross the Rubicon. Bowles decided to attack Panton's store six miles north of St. Mark's.

His partner, William Cunningham, walked into the Panton store and was greeted by the storekeeper, Edward Forrester. The two exchanged pleasantries—they had met a few times before when Cunningham accompanied Bowles to the store and attempted to woo Forrester away from Panton. The loyal clerk refused the bait—no hard feelings. This day, he even invited Cunningham to dine with him. The invitation was accepted.

As the meal was concluding, Cunningham leaped to his feet, drew his sword and proclaimed that Forrester and all gathered around the table were under arrest. Should anyone make a move, they would be gunned down by Bowles and his followers, who had the store surrounded. Panton's commissary now belonged to the director-general of the Muskogee Nation.[87]

Bowles entered the store and began to distribute the sought-after materiel, as well as boots, blankets and other items his Indian people might appreciate.

A few drinks in, Cunningham, who hated Spaniards with a passion ever since he served time in a Spanish prison for brigandry in East Florida, offered a reward for each Spanish scalp brought to him. The more sensible Bowles rescinded the order and had Cunningham tied up. Much to Bowles's chagrin—and later detriment—Cunningham escaped shortly after and made his way to the Spanish fort at San Marcos de Apalache.[88] Attempting to disassociate himself from—and avenge himself on—Bowles, Cunningham claimed to have been duped by the adventurer, who he did not realize had no official commission from Great Britain. In other words, he did not know that Bowles was acting on his own. (Given Cunningham's history as a vagabond and the likelihood that he had known Bowles for quite some time, the fort's commander placed Cunningham under arrest. He would eventually be sent as a prisoner to the Philippines, where he likely remained until his death.)[89]

The first stroke had gone as smoothly as possible. Next Bowles had to convince the Spaniards that he, not the despised and now impotent (or so Bowles claimed) Panton, was the man to deal with. He needed to convince the Spanish captain[90] who had been sent to Fort St. Mark, as well as Governor Carondelet in New Orleans, that Panton and McGillivray had exhausted their usefulness to His Majesty Carlos IV.

With the alliance with McGillivray still intact, Carondelet was at an impasse when it came to Bowles. Did he really represent the southern Creeks? If so, how many warriors did he really have at his disposal? What were his intentions? Prior to taking Panton's store, Bowles had sent a bombastic letter to the governor of Pensacola. He claimed that he only desired peace with Spain and that he had the means to procure said peace. The Creeks had united with the Cherokees and elected him their director-general. He had just dispatched 650 warriors to the coast where rivers running through Creek lands emptied into the Gulf. All he wanted from Spain was the right to free navigation of these rivers. His people needed access to cheaper trade goods. This demand was a matter of life and death. Deerskin prices had plummeted, and the Creeks needed the trade Bowles promised. Should Spain acquiesce, Bowles's warriors would help defend royal lands. Should Spain refuse, he would be forced to align the free state of Muskogee with the United States.[91]

Carondelet opted to invite Bowles to New Orleans to discuss his proposals. Surely Bowles must have had his suspicions. But then again, he had his pride. The Spanish governor of New Orleans was requesting a meeting with him. He, William Bowles, the director-general of the State of Muskogee, was being invited to the negotiating table of His Most Catholic Majesty Carlos IV's governor. Bowles was now a player on the world stage. Of course he agreed to the meeting.

On February 25, Bowles entered Fort St. Marks with only four bodyguards. (He had been told that he could bring as many as one hundred, but he

Hopothle Mico, or the Talassee King of the Creeks, by John Trumbull (1790). *New York Public Library.*

refused, confident that he had finally been accepted as the leader of the Creek Nation.) Once he rode into the fort, the commandant informed him that he would be going to New Orleans to finalize a treaty between Spain and Muskogee. Bowles asked to be able to return to camp to retrieve some papers, but the commander refused. The commandant told Bowles's four bodyguards that their leader would be taken by boat to meet with Carondelet. Bowles promised to return, and in the meantime, he placed co-conspirator Captain George Wellbank in charge of Muskogee.

The filibuster boarded his prison-boat on February 29. Distraught, his followers offered to exchange their prisoners and return the stolen Panton property in exchange for Bowles. The commandant refused, and on March 1, they set sail for New Orleans, arriving one week later.[92]

Across Four Continents
1792–1798

Carondelet treated his prisoner well but was unsure what to do with him. So, he passed him on to Governor Las Casas in Havana. Once in Cuba, Bowles was imprisoned in the infamous El Morro Castle. A few weeks later, he was sent on to Spain, where he was incarcerated until the Spanish government decided to send him off to the Philippines. He spent fifteen months in a Filipino jail and another two years as a prisoner in Manila, free to move about town but required to report each day to a magistrate, as well as feed, house and clothe himself.

In August 1797, Bowles was sent back to Spain. Along the way, he rallied some disgruntled sailors around him and tried to take over the ship. He failed and was sent aboard a French frigate that was convoying the Spanish ship to safety. Shortly after, a British frigate attacked, and during the melee, Bowles squeezed through a porthole, dove into the ocean and swam to an American ship nearby. From the safety of the American boat, Bowles taunted the French captain who had agreed to confine him: "I am now safe on shore and set down to tell you that your treatment to me on board the *Virtue* was extremely unjust and impolite…you ought [not] insult me in a public manner and treat me as a criminal.…I can never forgive and [unless you quickly apologize] shall mention you upon all occasions as a poltroon and a wreck."[93]

Bowles sailed with the Americans to British Sierra Leone, where he borrowed money for passage on a British ship headed to Tobago. The ship nearly sank during a terrific storm and had to be rescued by a British convoy heading to England. Bowles disembarked and was back in the country he had fought for during the American Revolution.[94]

Like he had in 1790, when Bowles had first visited London and found himself the toast of the town, dressing the part of the "noble savage," Bowles again flirted with London society in hopes of gaining British support for Muskogee. His argument was both simple and complex: Muskogee—and the twenty thousand warriors at Bowles's command—would be invaluable to Britain. With war looming with Spain, Spanish lands along the coast were up for grabs. Pensacola and St. Marks would provide Britain with strategic bases, ports and a leg up on the region's fur trade. New Orleans promised control of the Mississippi River, thereby providing a link between Canada and the Gulf Coast. Once dissatisfied American westerners broke with the United States and joined Great Britain, King George III would have a restored American empire, larger than ever. And then the Spanish lands in Mexico…and then Central America…and then South America. All it would cost His Britannic Majesty? Support of William Augustus Bowles and his State of Muskogee.[95]

London provided a handful of intoxicated admirers and well-wishers but no official sanction. Desperate to return to "his people," Bowles bought the cheapest passage he could find and set sail for his adopted homeland.

The Renegades

1799–1803, the End of the Muskogee
William Augustus Bowles

In 1799, Bowles was back in the Floridas with dreams of reestablishing his Muskogee state. When the new governor of Louisiana, Manuel Gayoso, learned that Bowles was once again on the loose, he sent Spanish ships to cruise the coast to keep Bowles out of Florida. There was the equivalent of a $4,500 reward for his arrest or head. Twenty riflemen and five Indians were hired to guard the mouths of potential rivers at which Bowles might land.[96]

None of these precautions worked. Not even a violent storm at sea that wrecked his boat could keep Bowles from Florida. On September 4, his boat wrecked on St. George Island, just off the Florida coast. He was found by a handful of Indians, who could not believe that the White adventurer had returned. Ironically, Joseph Ellicott, the famous surveyor, was on an adjacent island. Out of pity, he sailed a small boat loaded with provisions to the storm-battered passengers on St. George Island. Rough winds delayed Ellicott's return, and so he spent a week with Bowles. Bowles tried to convince the American surveyor that he had no animosity toward the United States, that the United States and the State of Muskogee were natural allies against the Spaniards. He told Ellicott that he would soon be in possession of Panton's store. In fact, he spoke openly and enthusiastically of the soon-to-be-powerful State of Muskogee. Ellicott was impressed with the fiery adventurer, but when he returned to Philadelphia, he urged the U.S. government to oppose Bowles at all costs. The man was clearly talented, courageous and charismatic. But he was also dangerous to the interests of the U.S. government.[97]

Back on the mainland, Bowles immediately began to rebuild his reputation among the Creeks. He played off their frustrations with Panton's exorbitant prices, as well as the niggardly gifts of the Spanish. He reminded them that when Britain had ruled the Floridas, the gifts had been both of better quality and more abundant. If only Panton was forced to flee and the Spanish yoke cast aside....

Bowles promised that he had been in contact with King George III, who wished to once again take the Creeks under his protection. When the adventurer handed out gifts—including several kegs of rum—it only lent credibility to his claims.

Spain had reason to fear Bowles. After five years in various prisons around the globe, there was little chance that Bowles would be anything but Spain's implacable enemy from here on out.[98]

In early 1803, Bowles once again marched on Panton's store. He claimed that the Scottish merchant was betraying his country by selling arms to the Spaniards in the midst of war and that he was abusing the natives by charging exorbitant prices. Enough Indians joined with Bowles that the few Whites and Indians defending Panton's store promptly withdrew. Bowles was once again master of the valuable warehouse.

With British smugglers in the vicinity, Bowles decided that he must take Fort San Marcos de Apalache itself.[99] Doing so would open the floodgates of trade between Nassau and Muskogee. The British would see the value in openly acknowledging the free state of Muskogee, with Bowles as its director-general. And more recruits would flock to Muskogee's standard once they saw the ineptitude of Spanish rule.

So, Bowles did indeed move against Fort San Marcos. He sent one of his followers to the fort's commander with the following declaration of war: "We pray God the great disposer of all things, who knows the wickedness of our enemies, who knows the justice of our Cause to favor our exertions.... God save Muskogee."[100]

The attack on San Marcos was Bowles's Rubicon. Previously, he could claim—and did claim—that he was working in the interests of King Carlos IV; that supporting Panton was bad business; and that he, Bowles, as elected

Right: *A Buccaneer*, by Alfred Rudolph (circa 1860). *Library of Congress.*

Below: Fort San Marcos. Historical marker on the interpretive trail at San Marcos de Apalache State Park.

leader, spoke on behalf of the Creek Nation. He had offered an alliance with Spain. Now he declared war. The end could only be glory or death.

On April 9, 1800, Bowles opened the siege against the Spanish fort. At his disposal he had several hundred Creek and Seminole warriors and a handful of White adventurers but no artillery. The fort contained twelve cannons and eighty-eight men. Bowles was attempting something previously unheard of: keeping a poorly armed Indian army in the field for weeks, possibly months, besieging a White fort, properly armed and well provisioned. The prospects looked glum for Bowles, but he was a gambler; now he was gambling that his charisma would hold his army together and that a relief force would not come to the fort in time.

But after three weeks, relief did come—in the form of a solitary supply ship, which was promptly captured by Bowles's navy. He now had enough provisions to keep his army in the field a few more weeks. Two weeks later, Panton's own ship, the *Sheerwater*, arrived carrying plenty of provisions and two cannons. To make certain that the fort was still in Spanish hands, the boat landed beneath the fort. The captain disembarked to investigate and was immediately captured by Bowles's Indians. Bowles himself then rowed out to the ship with six followers and overwhelmed the five-man crew. Bowles now had supplies and two cannons.

At last the Spanish commandant was willing to negotiate. He invited Bowles into the fort for peace talks. Remembering the last time he had entered San Marcos de Apalache for peace talks with Spain, Bowles demurred. Instead, the two met outside beneath a patch of pine trees.

Terrified that the newly acquired cannons might open a breach in his wall and visualizing hundreds of angry Indian warriors pouring through and torturing his soldiers—and wife, who was present—the commandant eventually agreed to surrender the fort. Bowles's terms were generous. He allowed the Spaniards to return to either New Orleans or Pensacola with their arms. All Bowles needed was the fort and its twelve cannons. On May 19, Spain surrendered its fort on the Apalachicola River. The Muskogee flag waved above Bowles as he watched triumphantly as the two Spanish vessels carrying nearly one hundred soldiers departed his nation. Bowles promptly sent news of his victory throughout the region, reminding recalcitrant Indians what he was capable of, urging White adventurers to flock to Muskogee and letting British merchants know that the free state of Muskogee was now open for business.[101]

Five weeks later, the Spanish flag was once again flying over San Marcos de Apalache. Governor Folch put together an army and, accompanied by a

Flag of the State of Muskogee. *Museum at San Marcos de Apalache State Park.*

fleet of armed ships, opened an intense bombardment. Bowles, who had few men capable of firing his own fourteen cannons, saw the writing on the wall and fled. Before fleeing, he loaded three boats with the captured goods, but these were recaptured by Folch the following day.

Once again, Bowles was on the run. Once again, he proposed a treaty with Spain. Once again, he was rebuffed. Bowles, who just five weeks before was a resurrected star, had now sunk into the abyss of the Gulf Coast power game. But the exuberant and optimistic director-general refused to despair. He understood that the fate of Muskogee would be decided in London. If Britain would invade the Gulf Coast, Muskogee—and he—would survive. But first Bowles needed to build another army.

BOWLES'S SCHEMES BEGAN TO wear on his opponents. He had increased the size of his navy and issued more letters of marque. His small flotilla attacked only Spanish shipping and did negligible—but noticeable—damage, causing the world's third-most powerful navy embarrassment. Furthermore, a Spanish treaty with the United States in 1795 stipulated that each nation was responsible for maintaining peace on its side of the border. Spain's inability to control the renegade Bowles was making some in America question the efficacy of Spanish rule in the Floridas. Already, many Americans were plotting ways to add more stars to the national flag. And then there was Indian agent Benjamin Hawkins, who was insisting that Bowles be removed from the region one way or another. Finally, even Bowles's British allies, particularly the merchants in Nassau who opposed the Panton, Leslie & Company monopoly, realized the futility of supporting the adventurer, who was proving to be nothing more than a nuisance and a dreamer. When a Muskogee privateer sailed into Nassau with a prize, the Admiralty Court refused to condemn the captured ship. Instead, the court declared the State of Muskogee a fiction and Bowles a dangerous charlatan.[102]

With even his British allies turning on him, Bowles's demise was only a matter of time. To ensure that Bowles could not retain the Indian allies he still had, Spain negotiated a separate peace with the Seminoles in 1802, and Pensacola governor Folch established a blockade of West Florida. If Bowles were unable to supply his followers with trade goods and war materiel, the last of his support would go dry. By now, British merchants were no longer willing to run the Spanish blockade to bring supplies to the charlatan. Meanwhile, Hawkins, Indians hostile to Bowles and Spanish authorities put a more definitive plan into action.[103]

Chapter 5

SLAVERY FROM AFRICA TO THE GULF COAST, 1528–1865

THE BLACKS

1528–1865, Africa, the Gulf Coast

One of the many great tragedies of slavery is the inevitable scant historical record. Deemed unworthy of formal education, as well as incapable of utilizing it or dangerous when educated, most enslaved people were unable to leave behind a written record. Consequently, few journals or memoirs exist telling the story of slavery from the slaves' perspectives. The handful that do exist provide invaluable insights into the nature of the peculiar institution. The following four vignettes come from different sources, telling the stories of four different persons who lived as slaves. Taken together, their story is representative of the millions of slaves who labored in the United States.

Capture

Prince Ibrahima, son of King Sori of the Fulbe, sat on the ground, sword hidden. A Heboh warrior approached and, noticing the prince's clothes, decided to capture and ransom him. He moved in to claim his reward. Ibrahima leaped to his feet: "I had a sword, but they did not see it. The first one that came, I sprang forward and killed."[104] A musket butt crashed against Ibrahima's head, and he lost consciousness.

Ibrahima, "Prince of Slaves." *Library of Congress.*

Ibrahima awoke submerged in a pond. The Heboh, having revived him, dragged him back to shore, where they stripped and bound the prince of Fulbe. "They made me go barefoot one hundred miles and led my horse before me."[105] Ibrahima knew the fate that awaited him. Being a powerful African prince, he had enslaved countless enemies himself. Now the tables had been turned. Ibrahima's one hope was that his father would arrive before the Hebohs sold him to Europeans or Americans.

King Sori did indeed immediately set out at the head of a powerful army to free his son. Unfortunately for Ibrahima, a handful of Mandinka *slatees* arrived as the Hebohs fled the wrath of Sori.[106] The *slatees* came from the Gambia River to buy slaves from the interior. They would lead their newly acquired slaves in coffles to coastal kingdoms, where they would realize a sizeable profit. The presence of the Mandinka was ominous. Ibrahima now knew that his father would not arrive in time. He had one last, desperate hope. He attempted to ransom himself, offering one hundred cattle, even more sheep and as much gold as one man could carry.[107] His captors would have none of it. Ibrahima was a hated enemy. He had killed and enslaved many Hebohs. As a contemporary English slave trader noted, "If they are captured that have been particularly active in wars—a King, Prince, or their sons—no price can purchase them."[108]

Ibrahima was sold for "two flasks of powder, a few trade muskets, eight hands of tobacco, and two bottles of rum."[109] The prince was on his way to the West African barracoons.

Barracoon

Kossola, a nineteen-year-old Isha[110] warrior, was marched into Dahomey, a prisoner of war. His village had been attacked by a rival king in the early morning hours. The elders had been decapitated on the spot, and the fit were taken away as slaves.

Kossola was marched by the house of Glele, the king of Dahomey. There he saw the heads of conquered tribes, including the fresh skull of his own chief:

> *Dey got de white skull bone on de stick when dey come meet us, and de men whut march in front of us, de got de fresh head high on de stick. De drum beat so much lookee lak de whole world is de drum dey beat on....*
>
> *Dey placee us in de barracoon* [stockade] *and we restee ourself. Dey give us something to eat, but not very much.*
>
> *We stay dere three days, den dey have a feast. Everybody sing and dance and beatee de drum.*[111]

A few days later, Kossola and his fellow Ishas were moved to the barracoon at Wydah, the infamous slave stockade in modern-day Benin. Over two centuries, the barracoons at Wydah held and then sold more than 1 million slaves, making it the second-largest slave trading port in Africa.[112] Each tribe was kept in separate stockades. Kossola, who had never heard the ocean or seen a White man, was exposed to both. The waves crashed against the shore day and night, and he could see White merchants going back and forth from ship to land.

The Slave Chain, depicting slavers and slaves in Dahomey, by Frederick E. Forbes (1850). *New York Public Library.*

Kossola knew that he was a prisoner, but he could not have yet known his fate. The White men he had been observing were in negotiations with the king of Dahomey to procure Kossola's labor for life:

> *When we dere three weeks a white man come in de barracoon wid two men of de Dahomey. One man, he a chief of Dahomey and de udder one his word-changer. Dey make everybody stand in a ring—'bout ten folkses in each ring. De men by dey self, De women by dey self. Den de white man lookee and lookee. He lookee hard at de skin and de feet and de legs and in de mouth. Den he choose.... [H]e take one hunnard and thirty....*
>
> *Den we cry, we sad 'cause we doan want to leave the rest of our people in de barracoon. We all lonesome for our home. We doan know whut goin' become of us, we doan want to be put apart from one 'nother.*[113]

The next day, Kossola and his 134 comrades were tied together and led to the waiting slave ship, the *Clotilda*.[114]

Across the Atlantic and the Gulf of Mexico

The transatlantic slave trade, in which 10 to 12 million Africans were shipped to the Americas as slaves, is well documented—the terrifying experience of boarding a floating house for the first time; the shackles and chains; being piled in like sardines; the vomit, urine and diarrhea sloshing back and forth; the never-ending rocking of the boat; the seasickness, the nausea, the unknown; the forced exercise on deck and the whips that encouraged the exercise; the return below decks; the chafing of the chains; the stench, sweat and excrement; the humiliation; the memories of freedom and home; and the despair. And at the end of the journey? The life of a slave.

As harrowing as the transatlantic slave trade was, the journey across the Gulf of Mexico was often just as bad. A journey of only two hundred miles from Pensacola to New Orleans could take up to three weeks due to suddenly shifting water levels and wind currents. A ship might be becalmed for days or weeks when the wind suddenly ceased. And then there were the pirates and hurricanes.

A journey from the West Indies to New Orleans was even more fraught with danger. Many slaves were sent more than one thousand miles to the Yucatan and then another seven hundred north to New Orleans or other ports along the Gulf Coast. Because intercolonial ships were not equipped to transport slaves, conditions were often worse than they were on the Middle Passage. After months of crossing the mid-Atlantic and months more

"View of Chained African Slaves in Cargo Hold of Slave Ship, Measuring Three Feet and Three Inches High" (nineteenth century). *New York Public Library.*

the Caribbean Sea and Gulf of Mexico, numerous slaves arrived at their new homes dispirited, exhausted and ill. The less fortunate were thrown overboard en route.[115]

Slavery

Between 1770 and 1808 (the legal closing of the foreign slave trade to the United States), nearly thirty thousand slaves were brought to New Orleans alone. Prior to 1803, most slaves came straight from Africa. After 1803—when America took control—about eleven thousand of the Crescent City's imported slaves were African-born (with more than one thousand coming from the Wydah slave market).[116] The rest came from either the domestic slave trade or slaves smuggled illegally by slavers and pirates. More slaves entered the United States through Pensacola, Mobile, Galveston and other smaller markets, both legally and illegally.

Slaves in the United States, whether native or imported from Africa, were familiar with the concept of slavery, for it had existed from time immemorial, both in Africa and in their new home. The extent of the misery of life as a slave was at the whim of the master, with some being more tolerant or more cruel than others. And yet most slaves shared similar experiences: uprootedness, fear of being sold, broken families, beatings, sexual advances, loss of control, little agency, drudgery, being reduced to chattel and dehumanization.

Countless anecdotes illustrate the dehumanizing side of life as a slave. One such anecdote follows:

> So mind I tell yo' what I seed wid my own eyes. De people take sick an' de die, dey ain't no coffin for dem, dey take planks an' nail dem together like a chicken coop—yo' can see through it, an' it's too short, de neck's too long. So a man stand up on him an' jump on him—here—he broke his neck, an' it fall on his chest like dis. Den dey nail de top on an' one nail go in de brain. I see dat wid my own eyes. Den dey put dem in de wagon what dey haul de manure in[,] nobody wid dem—de people have to go to work—wicked part o' de country—wicked! wicked! wicked![117]

As dehumanizing as slavery was, to both enslaved and slaver, the Gulf Coast was the last piece of U.S. soil to legally accept the bondage of human persons.[118]

Chapter 6

SPANISH-AMERICAN RELATIONS DETERIORATE, 1803–1810

THE SPANISH

Post-1803
Tensions with the United States following the Louisiana Purchase

The twenty-four crewmen of U.S. Gun-Boat No. 3 watched as the three tall-masted ships approached. Gun-Boat No. 3, sailing from New York, was passing through the Straits of Gibraltar—the narrow water route between Spain and Morocco that connected the Atlantic Ocean with the Mediterranean.

It was clear that the three approaching ships had ill intentions. As the ships drew nearer, the crewmen realized that these were Spanish privateers. Spain was not at war with the United States. Still, the privateers drew closer.

The crew of Gun-Boat No. 3 engaged. But ultimately, they were overwhelmed, boarded and steered north toward Spain. The crewmen soon found themselves prisoners in the Spanish port city of Algeciras. The American commander protested forcefully, and the Spanish authorities released the Americans and their ship shortly after. No one had been killed, but the diplomatic damage had been done.[119]

A few weeks later, an editorial appeared in a Natchez newspaper. The "nerveless Spaniard" was at it again. The capture of Gun-Boat No. 3 was only the latest in a series of affronts to the American character. But, the editorial concluded, "In the United States, every citizen is a soldier—every soldier a hero. Thus roused, and thus prepared, let Spain tremble for her colonial possessions."[120]

Victory at Gibraltar, by Petrus Johannes Schotel (circa 1850). *Rijksmuseum.*

SPAIN'S COLONIAL PORTFOLIO HAD taken a hit in the previous two years. At the turn of the nineteenth century, Spain had controlled New Orleans and Louisiana. Through effort, Spain had grown the population of Louisiana from 13,500 in 1769 to nearly 50,000 in 1799. Spain could exert significant control over Mississippi River traffic (although it had ultimately failed to stop Americans from navigating the river) and had hoped that Louisiana could be a populous, economically viable North American colony.

That hope had given way to disappointed pragmatism, and Spain signed Louisiana over to Napoleon Bonaparte's France in a secret treaty in 1800. Bonaparte wanted Louisiana to be a key part of its North American colonial holdings, along with San Domingue. After losing San Domingue to a slave revolt, Bonaparte's hopes for Louisiana vanished as well, and he sold the colony to the United States for $15 million in 1803.[121]

Spain found itself with a smaller empire—and neighbored suddenly by a United States actively expanding westward. And worse, for Spain, the United States claimed that its deal to buy Louisiana from France included sections of Spanish Mexico and Spanish West Florida. Louisiana, even at the time of the purchase, had been poorly mapped and explored.

Tensions between the United States and Spain rose, manifesting in different ways in different places. Spain feared losing the remainder of its north Atlantic empire, which included Mexico, the Floridas, Venezuela and Cuba. But the United States feared losing its newly acquired Louisiana territory to Spain as well. In the Atlantic, Spanish privateers harassed American ships. But on the western border of Louisiana, Spain prodded the United States in a different way.

In 1789, the Spanish king proclaimed that any foreign slave who escaped to Spanish territory would be set free. The law had gone unenforced. But with the Louisiana Purchase came a sudden enforcement of the law. Word spread among Louisiana's large population of enslaved Black people that freedom was just a short trip to Mexico away.

Spain had actively begun using the enslaved population of Louisiana as "informal agents in a much larger geopolitical struggle." A large-scale slave revolt was a real fear for the United States, especially after the recent uprising in San Domingue.

The undefined borders of Louisiana, as well as disagreements between Spain and the United States about which country owned which parts of the Floridas and Texas, meant that the people living in those places determined the borders in large part. The struggle could be seen playing out in real time in the American town of Natchitoches, on the western Louisiana border. Nearby was the similarly named Spanish town of Nacogdoches. A slave seeking freedom needed only to cross from one town to the other.

Within a year of the United States acquiring Louisiana, small-scale slave revolts and conspiracies had begun to form on the American side.

A View of New Orleans Taken from the Plantation of Marigny, by J.L. Boqueta de Woiseri (1803). *University of Wisconsin Milwaukee.*

In January 1806, a free Black man named Stephen informed American authorities that a plot had been set into motion for slaves in New Orleans to revolt en masse. The slaves would be joined by three or four thousand Spanish soldiers. High-ranking Spanish officials were supposedly involved in planning the insurrection. The insurrection never materialized on that scale, but the territorial governor of Louisiana, William C.C. Claiborne, took the threat seriously.

The issue drew the attention of U.S. Secretary of State James Madison, who requested that a subordinate negotiate with the Spanish to solve the problem. But the Spanish largely refused to act, leading to a military buildup along the border that almost led to a war in 1806.

In 1809, the Black population of Louisiana expanded significantly when about six thousand free and enslaved Black refugees, who had settled in Cuba but were originally from San Domingue, arrived. The influx of Black refugees further complicated American fears of a slave rebellion.

In 1811, a large-scale slave revolt finally materialized on Louisiana's German Coast when about five hundred slaves marched toward New Orleans. U.S. forces put down the revolt mercilessly. There was suspicion that Spain had orchestrated the rebellion.[122]

Beginning in 1810, revolutions in Spanish colonial holdings greatly weakened Spanish power in the Western Hemisphere. By 1820, Spain had ceded large amounts of its North American territory to the United States, and the amorphous borders of Louisiana had been defined and hardened.

The Renegades

May 25, 1803–December 1805
William Augustus Bowles

Tuckabatchee, Muskogee Nation[123]
May 25, 1803

Maryland-born William Augustus Bowles envisioned himself as the leader of a semi-autonomous Muskogee state under the protection of Great Britain. Since his youth, he had always been a loyal partisan of the British monarch. But he was also a proud member of a proud tribe. He had a pair of native wives and at least two Creek children. In short, he was proud to be White and proud to be Creek. Mostly, he was proud to be William Augustus Bowles. Therefore, it is no wonder that his overarching ambition, his dream, was to become the leader of a Muskogee state. He spent his life—he gave his life—in pursuit of this goal.

As he traveled to the great council at Tukabatchee in May 1803, dozens of plans raced through Bowles's mind. He would soon have the printing press that he had been planning for years (what respectable state could exist without making its proclamations known to the world?). He would soon have a formidable navy at his disposal, adding to the schooners he had fitted out as privateers that already flew the Muskogee flag. He would soon have a formal treaty that would allow his ships to carry the natural resources of Muskogee to foreign ports—most notably the Bahamas, but also to all nations at peace with Muskogee. He would soon have a number of ports, with their concomitant warehouses, from the Apalachicola to Tampa Bay, opened for foreign trade. White settlers would shortly begin coming to Muskogee to claim one hundred acres of free land. And the State of Muskogee would soon have its own university, its own army and its own independent government. Muskogee would be the first European-recognized Indian state in the New World.

The State of Muskogee had been germinating in the mind of William Augustus Bowles for a decade. Today, it would be realized.

By mid-May, the Upper and Lower Creek delegations had arrived. Other tribes, including the Cherokees and Seminoles, followed. Several White men soon joined, including U.S. Indian agent Benjamin Hawkins; Esteban Folch, the son of Pensacola's governor; and John Forbes, head of the Panton, Leslie & Company empire. Unbeknownst to Bowles, a conspiracy—not of his making—was afoot.

Told who was present, Bowles must have sensed danger. Nevertheless, he boldly walked straight to the council square and began denouncing the greedy Americans. Predicting that Hawkins and Folch would be "caught in their own trap," he urged the Indians to unite under the banner of Muskogee. He promised an independent Indian state within the protectorate of George III, on whose behalf he spoke and who would surely come to his subjects' aid.

Unfortunately for Bowles, King George III was no longer interested in his adventures. But President Thomas Jefferson, Secretary of State

Brig on the Water, by Gustave le Gray (1856). *Metropolitan Museum of Art.*

James Madison, Pensacola governor Folch and King Carlos IV of Spain were very much interested. The powers that be decided that Bowles must be eliminated.

Several Upper Creek, led by Sam Moniac and accompanied by Hawkins and Forbes, entered Bowles's tent and placed the director-general of the State of Muskogee in irons.[124] The filibustering career of William Augustus Bowles was at an end…or so it would seem.

BOWLES FLOATED DOWN THE Alabama River, a prisoner of the Creeks. Within a week, his captors expected to hand the filibuster over to Spain and receive their $4,500 reward.[125]

Four days after the capture, the Creeks and a still-bound Bowles camped on an island in the middle of the river. When they awoke in the morning, Bowles was gone, along with one of the pirogues. Shamed at losing their prisoner and fearing the loss of their reward, the panicked Indians began a desperate search for their escaped charge. Fortunately for them, they quickly found the pirogue on the other shore and followed Bowles's tracks. Once again, they apprehended the director-general of Muskogee and, this time, finished the journey, arriving in Mobile to collect their reward.[126]

Governor Folch immediately assigned six Spanish guards to Bowles and sent him by ship to New Orleans, as far away as possible from whatever allies Bowles might have left. By mid-June, Bowles was on his way to Havana, where he would again be incarcerated in Morro Prison.[127]

Two and a half years later, still awaiting trial, William Augustus Bowles died in the Morro Prison hospital.[128] Thus ended the saga of one of the most colorful, courageous and delusional figures in Gulf Coast history. Bowles dreamed of becoming a de facto king and then acted to make it happen. Again. And again. And again. The ever-youthful visionary pulled off—even for only the briefest of moments—what many thought could never happen (or would never allow to happen): an independent European-style Indian nation state.

THE AMERICANS (OR RENEGADES)

August 7, 1804, Baton Rouge
The Kemper Brothers

The Kemper brothers—Rueben, Nathan and Samuel—decided to move south and west. Again. Originally from Virginia, they followed the keelboats down the Ohio River. Rough, self-sufficient and educated, the trio decided to try their luck in the newly opened Mississippi Territory. Upon arrival, the Kempers realized that land was cheaper, better and more abundant across the border in Spanish territory. And so the brothers took the requisite oath and opened shop in the Bayou Sara settlement.[129] Headstrong and defiant, they soon found themselves in conflict with the local land surveyor and *alcalde* (mayor)—and by extension the Spanish governor, Carlos Grand-Pre. The Kempers quickly developed a reputation as agitators and sowers of discontent. Constant clashes with the authorities eventually led to open conflict, with the brothers swearing to defend their homestead with force. Against a determined Grand-Pre, and with not enough local support, the Kempers were exiled from Spanish territory. They grudgingly withdrew to the American side of the border.

"A Drawing Believed to Be the Store Owned by John Smith and Ruben Kemper in Bayou Sara, c. 1802." *West Feliciana Historical Society & Museum.*

But not for long. The Kempers were determined to avenge themselves on those they saw as their despotic persecutors. All three brothers had acquired an implacable and lifelong hatred of Spain. They began to formulate a plan to reclaim their lost land and strike a blow against His Most Catholic Majesty: they would establish a free and independent republic of West Florida.

THE KEMPER BROTHERS PLANNED to capture Governor Carlos de Grand-Pre and a handful of other valuable prisoners. They would then use the captives to negotiate the Spanish abandonment of Fort San Carlos at Baton Rouge. Such a coup, the brothers concluded, would encourage other Americans in Spanish West Florida to take up arms against the His Most Catholic Majesty. Inevitably, the United States would soon after annex the short-lived republic, making West Florida the eighteenth U.S. state.

Nathan and Samuel Kemper set out from Pinckneyville, just inside the Mississippi Territory, with thirty men on August 7, 1804. They carried with them a declaration of independence and a flag that they planned to raise above the fort at Baton Rouge.

Bayou Sara *alcalde* John O'Connor was captured without resistance. Shortly after, the brothers' nemesis, the surveyor Captain Vicente Pintado, was also captured sans resistance, although his house was burned to the ground. The Scotsman *alcalde* Alexander Stirling, owner of a twenty-thousand-acre plantation five miles north of St. Francisville, was the third prisoner of the night. With three noteworthy prisoners in tow, the Kempers' plan was moving smoothly.

Because of cleverly deployed dragoons along the road, news of the insurrection remained a secret until about seven o'clock that evening. A stunned Grand-Pre ordered his garrison to arms, sent out a call to the local militia (which included many Americans contentedly living under Spanish rule)[130] and sent a picket of twenty men a few hundred yards in front of the fort with orders to immediately raise the alarm when the rebel force arrived.

At about 5:30 in the morning, the Kempers' force arrived. Surprised and disappointed that their plot had finally been uncovered, the Kempers were now in a conundrum. They had promised their followers that hundreds more would flock to their ranks along the way—none had. They had also counted on a surprise attack to capture Grand-Pre. Now their plan was in shambles. And yet, to retreat at this point would be an unmitigated failure.

Bayou Sara in the 1840s, by Lewis Henry (1857). *Wikimedia Commons.*

Should the current attempt fail, there might not be another. Dreams of a West Florida republic would remain just that.

Samuel ordered his men to fire on the picket. Two Spaniards fell wounded, and the picket retreated to the safety of the fort. The rebels had now fired on government troops. There would be reprisals. It was imperative that the Kemper brothers emerge from their fiasco with some credibility. Yet they were outmanned and had no artillery. Storming the fort was out of the question.

And so Samuel decided to negotiate. He sent one of his hostages, John O'Connor, to Grand-Pre with the following offering: the Kempers would release their three high-profile prisoners in exchange for a handful of American prisoners being held in Baton Rouge. (These prisoners had been early supporters of the Kempers when the brothers first began to actively resist Spanish officials and surveyors.) Grand-Pre refused to even enter into negotiations with the rebels, as doing so would have acknowledged their legitimacy.

With their offer rebuffed and Spanish reinforcements on the way, the Kemper brothers were out of options. They kept their force of thirty men within sight of the fort for a day and then withdrew to the border. When Spanish troops pursued, the Kempers made as if to resist but eventually retreated back to Pinckneyville in U.S. territory.

Word quickly spread throughout the two empires—the established Spanish and the burgeoning American. Naturally, Spain saw the Kemper expedition as a direct assault on sovereign Spanish territory and called for the United States to arrest and hand over the perpetrators. Through various diplomatic avenues, the United States delayed, made excuses and ultimately refused to arrest the Kempers. Meanwhile, American papers were filled with the daring exploits of the Kemper brothers and their band of patriots—on both sides of the border—and their bold fight against the despotic Spanish dons. The papers portrayed the Spanish southwest as oppressed, discontent and ripe for the picking.

The reality of West Florida, however, was startlingly different. For the most part, Americans living under Spanish rule were content. William C. Davis explained:

> *The rhetoric of liberty more than once masked a thirst for plunder, and the efforts of Americans settlers to halt such activity shows how little most of it had to do with American nationalism. The raiders, whatever their initial motivation, were opportunists, with too many lies and too much plundering*

to sustain an image of freedom fighters. Most Americans in West Florida already had as much freedom as they wanted, and more than they would have if the United States took over, at least when it came to deserters, fugitives from civil justice, and debtors hiding from creditors. Some preferred Spanish indolence and inefficiency in government to the more active justice system that might be imposed by the Americans. Land was still cheap or even free and easily available from Spain, whereas in the United States' territories, the speculators seemed to get the best tracts first. British inhabitants to the province and the Tories who had fled there from the Revolution were already conditioned to be loyal to a distant monarch, so Spain's king represented nothing unusual; what the Kempers offered would only return them to the political system they had come there to escape. Men act in self-interest, and the Kempers learned the hard way that the interest of most Americans at the moment simply did not mirror their own.[131]

The first attempt to establish an independent West Florida Republic had been an abject failure. It would not be the Kemper brothers' final attempt.[132]

The Americans (or Renegades)

September 23, 1810, Baton Rouge
Philemon Thomas and Isaac Johnson

As soon as American lands abutted Spanish territory on the southwestern frontier, Americans began to plot and scheme ways to add the "Donnish" lands to their own ever-expanding nation. The Kempers' failure in 1804 failed to dissuade other would-be filibusters.

By 1810, the anti-Spanish conniving had reached a crescendo. Mississippians and Louisianans, considering themselves patriotic Americans and inheritors of the Revolutionary spirit, determined to carve out an independent republic at the expense of Spain. They would foment a rebellion that would lead to the establishment of the West Florida Republic. Shortly thereafter, the revolutionaries would hand their republic over to the United States.

In effect, insurrectionists, acting independently of the United States, would do the will of the United States and conquer what their native land had lusted after ever since its birth twenty-seven years before.

A mansion at the Myrtles Plantation in St. Francisville, Louisiana, constructed around 1796. The mansion existed within the short-lived West Florida Republic. *Library of Congress.*

The expedition would fall under the command of General Philemon Thomas and Major Isaac Johnson. Like Rueben Kemper, Thomas was a grocer, as well as an innkeeper. Gruff, likeable and brave, the forty-six-year-old Virginian and veteran of the American Revolution was a natural-born leader. Now living near Baton Rouge, the colorful shopkeeper went from promoting "akomidation fur Man & Beest" and "coughphy for sail" to being one of the principal leaders of the West Florida rebellion.[133] Isaac Johnson had been a former surveyor on the Spanish side of the border and had a working relationship with the "Dons." However, by 1810, his allegiance lay entirely with the rebels. So did his wife's. While Johnson prepared his men for the confrontation ahead, his wife, Melissa, set about sewing a standard for her husband's men to follow. She presented Isaac with a blue cloth flag with a single white star in its middle.[134] (Melissa Johnson's flag would serve as the banner of the West Florida rebellion and as the standard for a much larger rebellion forty-one years later.)

Like Galvez thirty-one years before, the American insurgents decided to attack Fort San Carlos by using the overlooked river road. Unlike Galvez, they would attack from St. Francisville to the north. Convinced that if an attack occurred at all it would be from the plain to the east, the new Spanish governor, Charles de Hault Delassus, ordered a guard and two cannons facing east. The governor had been warned that afternoon there had been suspicious activity all morning in St. Francisville, and it looked as if an attack was imminent. Nevertheless, Delassus returned to his own house in town after posting a guard of eight men under the son of former governor Carlos de Grand-Pre, Luis, and three sentinels.

After rendezvousing in St. Francisville, Thomas and Johnson had at their disposal seventy-five soldier/adventurers. Fort San Carlos housed twenty-eight soldiers, of whom a handful were in the infirmary, and a dozen functioning cannons. Fearing the latter, Thomas decided to take the fort by stealth. Familiar with the river road, Thomas was reassured when one of his men, Larry Moore, a Kentuckian living in Spanish territory, told him he had seen cows moving back and forth from the fort to the river. "Ef them cows kin git in thar an' outen again, I knows my pony kin tote me in the same way, an' do h'it as easy as fallin' offen a log."[135]

The Americans arrived outside the fort, undetected, around three o'clock in the morning. With Spanish eyes looking east and a light fog hovering over the ground, the invaders formed a line along the river road and quietly marched forward. Finally, a sentry heard a horse approaching outside the fort. He squinted through the mist and saw a band of fog-enshrouded cavalry riding toward the still open gate. "Who goes there?" No answer. "Here they come!" the surprised sentinel called out to his mostly sleeping comrades.

The Americans stormed the gate, with Thomas, not knowing that the governor was between his house and the fort, calling out to Delassus in

Sea Fight (anonymous, late seventeenth century). *Rijksmuseum.*

Grave of General Philemon Thomas in Baton Rouge, Louisiana. *Library of Congress.*

his native tongue, "Ground your arms and you shall not be hurt." He had previously told his men not to fire unless fired on, and now they rushed into the fort shouting, "Hurrah! Washington!"

Luis Grand-Pre rallied his men from the guardhouse and formed them in a line. Seeing only the cavalry of the Americans, he believed that he had an advantage, drew his sword and marched alone toward the American cavalry demanding their surrender. At that moment, the second contingent of Americans under Major Johnson rushed through the front gate, behind the Spaniards. Now surrounded, the impetuous Grand-Pre ordered his men to fire. One, two, three muskets cracked from the frightened and ill-prepared Spaniards. The Americans retaliated with a much more concerted, deadlier volley of their own. Five Spaniards fell—one dead, two mortally wounded. Grand-Pre himself was hit with five musket balls, including a deadly one lodged in his kidney. Covered in blood, the brave but foolish Grand-Pre fell to the ground. Meanwhile, his terrified fellow soldiers were tossing down their arms in surrender.

As the first shots pierced the early morning air, Governor Delassus, already on his way back to the fort, broke into a sprint. When he arrived at the gate and took in the scene, the stunned governor shouted, "Alas, what is this?" Rebel cavalry seized him where he stood. The rebels began demanding his sword, and when Dealassus refused to formally surrender, a musket butt knocked him to the ground. Thomas intervened—probably saving the governor's life—and ordered his men to secure the fort. Major Johnson soon found the flag of Castile and Leon and began dragging it through the dirt of the parade ground. Above the stained and tattered flag of Spain fluttered the new flag of Fort San Carlos and Baton Rouge: the lone star of the Republic of West Florida.[136]

TWO AND A HALF months later, U.S. troops marched on Fort San Carlos, which now waved the flag of the Republic of West Florida. After a brief negotiation, the insurgents agreed to hand the fort (and the republic) over to American forces. Baton Rouge was now an American possession. Naturally, Spain resisted the conquest of its territories and refused to acknowledge either the Republic of West Florida or the stars and stripes that now waved above the fort and town.

The fate of West Florida and the American southwest would hinge on yet another war brewing throughout the Gulf Coast.

Chapter 7

THE SLAVES FIGHT BACK, 1811

THE BLACKS

January 8, 1811, German Coast
Charles Deslondes, Kook, and Quamana

Charles Deslondes gathered his men outside the plantation home of Manuel Andry. The rain helped conceal the slaves as they ran toward the back door, cane knives and machetes in hand. They barged in and ascended the double staircase to the rooms of Manuel and his son Gilbert. Manuel arose to see his trusted overseer, Charles Deslondes, axe in hand, moving toward him. Thinking quickly, Manuel leaped from his bed and charged the stunned slaves, who slashed at him with axe and blades, wounding him seriously. Still, Manuel ran on toward the staircase, not stopping but glancing over to see slaves hacking his son Gilbert to death. The terrified Manuel Andry ran across his fields to a waiting pirogue and made his escape. Three days later, Andry would write to Governor Claiborne, "My poor son has been ferociously murdered by a horde of brigands who from my plantation to that of Mr. Fortier have committed every kind of mischief and excesses, which can be expected from a gang of atrocious bandittis of that nature."[137]

The "bandittis of that nature" were not ignorant savages from Africa or San Domingue, as many planters assumed. They were not docile field hands in need of a paternalistic master to survive. They were not a spurof-the-moment assembly of savages. Instead, they were a well-organized army of several hundred soldiers, with flags and weapons, and some in military uniform. Their plot had been brewing—unnoticed by the ever-watchful Whites—for months. Despite a system that rewarded, and survived, off paid informants among the slaves, no one betrayed the coup. The "ignorant savages" had plotted, organized and set in motion a rebellion that now threatened New Orleans itself.

BLOW FOR BLOW.

Blow for Blow, by H.L. Stephens (1863). *Library of Congress.*

After taking over the Andry plantation, Deslondes's army was not satisfied. The goal was not revenge but freedom. The slaves raided the plantation armory, a handful putting on the stored militia uniforms. They began the march south en masse, chanting "On to New Orleans!," where Deslondes hoped to establish an independent Maroon nation.

The march took the slave army down the River Road, along the Mississippi levee. Word of the revolt spread quickly, and roughly one-fourth of the slaves along the path joined Deslondes's army.[138] Past mansions and slave quarters and sugar trees, closer and closer to New Orleans they marched in military formation, an African drum setting the pace. In two days, they would be in New Orleans.

Five miles down the River Road, the slaves were met by reinforcements— ten slaves from the Trouard plantation led by a mounted slave named Mathurin. Mathurin would be the first of a number of mounted slaves who would form the cavalry of the army. However, the master, Achille Trouard, had been tipped off by a loyal slave and escaped into the swamps. Whereas the rebellion began in secrecy, evidently word spread quickly among the White community as well. Deslondes could now expect stiffer resistance the rest of the way.

And yet resistance never materialized that first day of the revolt. Several slaves, when they heard of the revolt, warned their masters. Nearly all the White planters chose to flee rather than resist. As a result, Deslondes's army marched the first ten miles of the route with no opposition—just empty plantations. While most slaves chose to shun the rebels, enough joined to create a formidable army. When Deslondes reached the Brown plantation, two experienced Akan warriors, Kook and Quamana, and their twenty-five followers rallied to Deslondes, who by now had more than two hundred men and eleven cavalry in his army.[139]

Burning buildings along the way—not as many as they planned due to rain and lack of time—the slave army continued its inexorable march toward New Orleans unopposed—that is, until they came to the plantation of Francois Trepangier. Having been warned by a loyal slave (or a slave looking to be rewarded down the road), Trepangier sent his weeping wife and family into the swamps, despite her protestations to accompany them. After all, what was there to fear from a handful of Africans? Trepangier awaited their arrival on his second-floor balcony, shotgun in hand. To his dismay, Deslondes's army turned the corner in military formation, led by officers, flags flying. Trepangier opened an ineffective fire while one detachment began to build a fire at his mansion's foundations. Meanwhile, the giant Kook led another detachment up the back stairs. As Trepangier fired away, Kook burst into his room and hacked him to death with an axe.[140]

The slave army had claimed its second victim, and it was thirsty for more as the sun began to rise over the German Coast, a land where slaves far outnumbered their masters.

An abandoned mansion near Destrehan, Louisiana (1938). *Library of Congress.*

Deslondes was now less than twenty-five miles from New Orleans. He had good reason to believe that his army would continue to grow as word of its success preceded him. White planters would continue to flee, and slaves would swell his numbers. With the American army off in Baton Rouge to guard against a Spanish threat, New Orleans was especially vulnerable. If Deslondes successfully stormed the city, he could establish a colony to which slaves all over the South would flock. A new Haiti—a Black, independent republic established on the southern tip of the United States. If only he could reach New Orleans. If only his fellow slaves would join him.

But they didn't. At least not as many as he had expected. Most of the slaves preferred security and life to potential freedom coupled with potential death. And so the Black leaders began to threaten with death any slave who failed to join their ranks.[141] While most resisted, handfuls here and there joined the rebellion. Ransacking two plantations along the way, the troop arrived at the Kenner plantation, fifteen miles outside New Orleans, and within sight of the cathedral spire and ships' masts in the harbor.

Unseen by the slave army, an army of equal size was presently planning a counterattack.

Whereas only half the slaves were armed with functioning guns (the other half carried scythes and knives), the Americans faced no such shortage. After locating the rebel army, General Wade Hampton (who had arrived two days before to help fight the Spanish in West Florida) ordered a surprise three-pronged assault on the camp. But when the American cavalry and soldiers burst into the camp, they found it deserted. Alerted by scouts, the Black leaders had quietly slipped away with their entire army, leaving the American army bewildered.

Unfortunately for Kook, Quamana and Deslondes, a second army was presently crossing the swift-moving Mississippi River to their north.

After his miraculous escape, Manuel Andry arrived at a friend's plantation with his horrifying tale. The planter rallied roughly eighty fellow Whites—mostly of French stock—to his side, and not trusting the American army, he determined to kill or capture the slaves himself.

As Deslondes was leading his force north, the planters, who had landed farther north, were marching south, hoping to catch the rebel army. Not knowing that he now faced two armies, in front and behind, Deslondes was stunned when he encountered eighty White men, armed to the teeth, in his line of march. The two sides quickly formed in the rain and marched toward each other. At several hundred yards apart, loud *cracks* split the air. Smoke immediately obscured everything between the two armies, and bullets whizzed by like angry bees. Men shouted and screamed in varying dialects. Limp bodies dropped and thudded against the muddy ground.[142]

After quickly expending their limited ammunition, the slaves fled to the safety of a cypress swamp, mounted planters in pursuit. A Spanish spy in New Orleans later reported to his government, "Fifteen or twenty of them were killed and fifty prisoners were taken including three of their leaders with uniforms and epaulets. The rest fled quickly into the woods."[143] The massacre commenced. The wounded were put to death. The captured were returned to slavery. The ringleaders were saved for the next day.

Forty to forty-five slaves lay dead or dying on the marshy field. Several heads were promptly removed and delivered to the Andry estate. The rest were hung on poles as an example. Within three weeks, more than one hundred Black heads and mutilated bodies were hung at intervals from the Place d'Armes to forty miles distant along River Road—the same road the slaves had taken in hopes of taking New Orleans.

Charles Deslondes and a handful of slaves escaped into the swamps. The wounded were soon run down and dispatched or captured by a force of twenty-five planters and Indians, experienced in the ways of the swamp. More effective than even the Indians was a pack of bloodhounds, trained to hunt down fugitive slaves and Maroons.

The hounds quickly picked up the scent of Deslondes and began the inevitable pursuit. Deslondes ran, but the hounds ran faster. Louder and louder, closer and closer they came as the terrified slave who had known freedom for at least a day ran deeper into the swamp. He didn't get too far. The dogs pounced on him and began tearing apart his flesh. The hunters looked on until one recognized the leader of the failed rebellion. Only then did they call off the dogs. Deslondes was taken back to the battlefield to be made a public example/spectacle. The potential Toussaint Louverture had his hands chopped off and thighs broken before being shot to death. His body was then burned until only his ashes remained.[144]

Kook and Quamana were two of twenty-one prisoners who were marched south to the Destrehen plantation to be tried and executed as an example to other would-be slave rebels. The veneer of a trial would place the planters on the side of the civilized. The men who had just decapitated, mutilated and displayed dead bodies would show the world the superiority of their society to that of the Blacks who had murdered and rampaged their way along River Road.

Upon interrogation, several of the slaves immediately began denouncing their fellow warriors, especially Kook and Quamana. (Author Daniel Rasmussen pointed out the irony, universality and complexity of the rebellion: "During the interrogations, the slaves identified eleven separate leaders. These leaders came from Louisiana, from the Kongo, from the Asante kingdom, and even from white fathers. Their names were French, German, Spanish, West African, and Anglo-American.")[145] On the second day of the trial, Kook and Quamana were brought forth. Both refused to turn on their fellow freedom fighters. Both admitted to being leaders of the rebellion, with Kook admitting to the slaying of Trepagnier. Both received the same sentence: "CONDEMN[ED] to death without qualification....The heads of the executed shall be cut off and placed atop a pole on the spot where all can see the punishment meted out for such crimes, also as a terrible example to all who would disturb the public tranquility in the future."[146]

Along with eighteen others, Kook and Quamana were summarily shot to death. Their heads were cut off and joined the long line of poles raised for public viewing. Their souls floated away, joining a long line of freedom-seeking martyrs.

Chapter 8

AMERICAN PIRATES, 1810–1812

THE RENEGADES

1810–1812, Barataria
Pierre and Jean Laffite

With war raging in San Domingue, two of New Orleans's most colorful and controversial characters arrived in the Crescent City. By the time the brothers Laffite left a decade later, they had left an indelible mark on the city that would always be associated with their name and legend. The brothers helped romanticize piracy, brought desperately sought-after merchandise into a city suffering from an embargo, provided essential resources and advice at the Battle of New Orleans, perpetuated untold miseries through their slave smuggling operation and became the dichotomy of the hero/villain that so defines New Orleans.

In 1808, THE INTERNATIONAL slave trade was officially banned by the United States. The domestic trade was allowed to continue, but the importation of foreign slaves was forbidden. And yet the demand for slaves had skyrocketed since Eli Whitney's invention of the cotton gin fourteen years before. The unscrupulous saw opportunity: limited supply and exponential demand.

There was no such restriction on importing slaves in Spanish Pensacola, where San Domingue–born merchant Pierre Laffite attended a slave auction. The exorbitant prices made him realize how much American Louisianans

Portrait of Jean Laffite. *From the exhibit* Pirates!: Legends of the Gulf Coast Museum, *Galveston, Texas.*

would pay for slaves. The young opportunist contacted his brother, Jean, with a plan to smuggle slaves from Spanish territory into the United States using backroads and bayous.

The elder Laffite then moved his operation to New Orleans.[147]

REUNITED WITH HIS BROTHER Jean, Pierre became half of one of the most renowned smuggling operations in U.S. history.

Jean quickly established a smuggling colony on Grand Terre Island, south of New Orleans in the Barataria wetlands. The brothers Laffite would act as middlemen, bringing in buyers to their base where warehouses and barracoons had been built. The brothers also smuggled desirable goods into New Orleans itself. Being the go-between suited the brothers. After all, a smuggler/merchantman was a much safer profession than a privateer/pirate.

So successful was the brothers' operation that Pierre openly (and legally) bought a house in the French Quarter on St. Ann Street, where Jean was welcome whenever he came to town.[148] The Laffite racket was so successful—

and welcome—that the duo and their associates quickly became the toast of the community.

Ironically, it was President Jefferson who helped catapult the Laffites and other Gulf pirates into notoriety. While denouncing piracy—and even invading an African nation in an attempt to put an end to the Barbary pirates—Jefferson inadvertently encouraged the practice by placing an embargo on British goods in 1807, thereby making merchandise scarce and expensive. Pirates and smugglers helped alleviate much of this inflation. And so, when Jefferson sent his trusted seaman David Porter to the Gulf to curtail the pirates, he sent his master commandant into a prickly situation. Porter would report, "As they spent their money freely, the local authorities rather encouraged their presence. These desperadoes, mixing with the dissolute part of the population, kept the town in a continual state of turmoil."[149] He would later write, "The district attorney evidently winked at piracies committed in our waters and at the open communication kept up between these depredators and the citizens of New Orleans."[150]

The presence of American warships in the Gulf did little to endear the United States to New Orleans residents. Nor did it curtail smuggling to any noticeable degree. Pierre continued to operate with near impunity, and the ever-charming Jean drank and danced and made many important political connections in the process. Considering that of New Orleans's 24,552 residents in 1810, only 3,200 were English or American, it should come as no surprise that most residents preferred men like the Laffites to the likes of the American governor Claiborne or U.S. embargo enforcers.[151] And when men—be they smugglers, legitimate privateers or outright pirates—brought in much sought-after merchandise, and at discount prices, the populace tended to look the other way.

Even with smuggling widespread along the coast, the Laffites distinguished themselves as especially adept middlemen on Barataria. Privateers and pirates preferred to unload their wares quickly, and so the brothers were able to buy cheap. (Because of the embargo, they were able to sell high—but still low enough to ensure a steady clientele.) In addition to business savvy, Jean also had invaluable knowledge of the smuggling routes into the city—the nine- to ten-foot-deep passes were deep enough for his smugglers but too shallow for pursuing warships. It seemed that everyone enjoyed the largesse bestowed by the Laffites. Visitor and renowned engineer Arsene Lacarriere Latour reported, "The most respectable inhabitants of the state, especially those living in the country, were in the habit of purchasing smuggled goods coming from Barataria."[152]

"EL AGUILA DEL MAR"

¿A QUIÉN no le gustan las películas de asunto marino y de piratas? Nueva Orleáns, la ciudad que aún mantiene la influencia europea, el bello puerto del Atlántico, es la escena de este film.

Presentado por
ADOLPH ZUKOR
y
JESSE L. LASKY

con
FLORENCE VIDOR
RICARDO CORTEZ

Spanish-language advertisement for the silent film *The Eagle of the Sea*, in which Ricardo Cortez plays "Captain Sazarac," based on Jean Laffite (1927). *Internet Archive.*

So successful were the brothers at bringing illegal goods into their adopted city that they decided to expand their business into the slave market. Recalling the experience at the slave market in Pensacola, Pierre and Jean decided to earn serious money…and suffer serious punishment if caught. They would add slave running to their list of transgressions.

In the summer of 1810, Pierre sold nineteen slaves for $7,903—including one from San Domingue, one from Cuba and twelve fresh from Africa, a clear violation of the 1808 international slave ban. Over the next seven months, he made more than $12,000 from selling slaves.[153] Half a year later, in March and April 1811, he sold another twenty-five slaves (mostly from Africa) for $15,275.[154] So successful were the brothers that they bought a warehouse on Royal Street.

And then war between the United States and Britain erupted in 1812—a privateer's dream, a smuggler's fantasy.

Chapter 9

THE AMERICANS FLEX THEIR MUSCLE, 1813–1814

THE AMERICANS

1813
General Wilkinson Sacks Mobile

Readers of the *Mobile Gazette* opened their newspapers in mid-April 1813 to read confirmation of what they must have already known: the United States had captured their city. "GOOD NEWS," the headline read. "MOBILE TAKEN! PROCLAMATION!"

The proclamation printed that day was written by none other than General James Wilkinson, the American commander who had led the assault on Mobile. Wilkinson, writing from a camp outside Mobile, wanted to reassure the residents of Mobile that they would be safe as the United States occupied the city and that their property would remain safe: "Be not alarmed by appearances, but rest tranquil within your dwellings, and take no part in the scenes which may ensue the display of the American Standard in your vicinity."

Mobile, a vestige of Spanish power along the Gulf Coast, had been captured by the United States and was officially part of the Mississippi Territory. The inhabitants of Mobile who did not wish to live in that territory could leave; anyone who stayed would be subject to be laws of the United States.[155]

In the next few weeks, details of the cunning operation that wrested Mobile from Spanish hands were published in newspapers around the United States. From the beginning, secrecy was the priority of General Wilkinson, who received orders to advance on Mobile the month before.

Wilkinson, from headquarters in New Orleans, would have to draw together and organize troops, supplies and ships and set the operation in motion—all without alerting the Spanish, who controlled not only Mobile but also Pensacola. He sent a battalion of soldiers from the English Turn to Pass Christian—in present-day Mississippi—under the guise of a trip to preserve the health of the troops. He ordered artillery to the fort of Petite Coquille at the Rigolets under the guise of a fortification-building mission. He directed gunboats to Mobile Bay, where they could intercept any communication with Pensacola. He sent a communiqué to an American garrison at Fort Stoddert, north of Mobile—*be ready to march on Mobile immediately*.

Wilkinson left New Orleans on March 29, 1813, intending to collect and mobilize the troops, ships and artillery he had planted along the Gulf Coast in the previous weeks. The mission got off to a bad start when the barge Wilkinson was traveling on capsized on the way to Pass Christian. Wilkinson and the "half-drowned" crew of the barge were ironically rescued by a party of Spanish fishermen, who helped the party repair their boat and set off again toward Mobile.

Wilkinson rendezvoused with the other members of the expedition at Pass Christian, where they loaded thirty scaling ladders—crafted with precision to the exact height of the walls of Mobile—onto their ships. Wilkinson sent word to the troops stationed north of Mobile to start descending the river and occupy the bank on the east side of the city. The general, aboard the "armed boat Alligator," led the expedition out of Pass Christian and toward Mobile on April 7. Several transport ships accompanied him.

One boat was sent to draw off Spanish guards at Dauphin Island. With the way cleared, the American flotilla entered Mobile Bay around dusk. Throughout the night, six hundred American troops disembarked and formed a column. The next morning, they marched on Mobile and took positions in a wood outside the city.

Wilkinson sent a demand to the Spanish commandant inside the city demanding that he surrender the city and evacuate. He promptly did. Mobile had been captured without a battle. The success of the mission was due to Wilkinson's careful, and secretive, planning in the lead-up to the operation.[156]

The Indians

August 30, 1813, Fort Mims
Dixon Bailey, Creek Métis

Dixon Bailey, a Creek *métis*,[157] waited inside Fort Mims. Rumors of an imminent Red Stick Creek attack had permeated the region and sent White and Creek residents scurrying to the protection of stockades up and down the Mobile-Tensaw River Delta.[158]

Bailey knew that civil war was inevitable. The Creek Nation had divided. Those of the old school, the Red Stick faction, were determined to stand with the philosophy of Tecumseh—all-out resistance to the encroaching Americans. Others, like Bailey's family, stuck to the conservative religion of the Creeks but were more amenable to the fluid economic system introduced by Whites. Bailey, like so many other Creeks, tried to navigate both worlds. No doubt, economically, he was a success. The Creeks of the Tensaw were flourishing. Perhaps too much. The resistant-minded Creeks decided to teach the accommodationists a lesson. They began to heavily tax those Creeks who had begun to flourish by adopting American ways. Four years earlier, one such tax force under the command of Captain Sam Isaacs arrived at Bailey's house while he was out hunting. Isaacs asked the ferryman, Linn McGee, if Bailey intended to pay the tax/extortion, to which McGee replied, "No."

Tensaw resident Dr. Thomas G. Holmes related what happened when Bailey suddenly returned:

> [Bailey,] *fearless of all men, rushed upon* [Isaacs], *knocked him down.* [Soon surrounded] *by Isaacs warriors with their tomahawks one after another he laid them out. one fellow getting behind him, about striking him with a tomahawk.* [Just then, Dixon's sixty-year-old mother, Mary, arrived and] *seized the fellow around the middle & with a fortunate exertion threw him into the river. the indian carry the woman with him—one trying to drown the other. They both got to shore & crawled out. By this time Bailey had concurred Isaac & his men they were glad to retire.*[159]

The last four years had done nothing to mitigate the Creek culture war. The Tensaw had become a powder keg. And now Dixon Bailey anxiously awaited the outcome of the cultural turned physical war between the past and the future, inside a farm turned fort, next to a swamp turned farm, with a little more than five hundred persons, many Creek turned…whatever the new breed of Creek hoped to be.

Warnings of Red Stick sightings began trickling and then flooding into the fort. Major Daniel Beasley did his best to squelch rumors. One slave who had reported the potential war party while attending cattle beyond the walls was publicly scourged. The next day, the same slave again saw Red Stick warriors within a mile of the fort. This time he ran off to another fort, five miles to the southeast. His fellow slave and helper hurried back to Fort Mims, where he spread the alarm. He, too, was given thirty-nine lashes for his loyalty.

Dixon Bailey and the five hundred other fidgety Whites, slaves and *métis* looked on and wondered how they would react if the Red Sticks did attack.

Meanwhile, seven hundred Creek warriors lay concealed in a ravine four hundred yards to the east. At a prearranged signal, the warriors stormed the fort. They ran unnoticed by the poker-playing sentry until they were only thirty yards away. Two more columns of Red Sticks stormed the gun holes on the outer walls. Dixon Bailey joined the militia and other *métis* at the northern wall. It quickly became apparent that the fort was fatally flawed. The gun holes were only three to four feet high, enabling both those inside and outside the fort to fire behind cover. (Had the gun holes been built at six or seven feet, only the defenders would have been able to access them from atop a raised earthen mound inside the fort.) The Red Stick strategy to take control of the bulk of the gun holes effectively doomed Fort Mims. Those inside began to pack inside the dozen small buildings inside the fort.

Realizing the danger of their position—as well as the consequences of losing the fort—the militia and the Creek *métis* fought with desperate abandon. Dixon Bailey held his post at the north wall, while his fifteen-year-old brother, Daniel Bailey, and a few others climbed into the attic of Samuel Mims's house and began removing shingles. From their new position, they opened an effective fire on the northern and southern fields. At two o'clock in the afternoon, the Red Sticks withdrew and held a council of war at a cabin northeast of Fort Mims. The debate raged as hotly as the battle had for nearly an hour. Ultimately, it was determined that the battle would continue. Heavy losses had already been inflicted on the fort's White defenders, but so far the *métis*—the Creek accommodationists—

Left: Blockhouse at Fort Mims. *Collection of Ryan Starrett.*

Below: Palisades at Fort Mims. *Collection of Ryan Starrett.*

were relatively unscathed. Until Dixon Bailey and his fellow *métis* ("traitor Creeks") were sufficiently punished, preferably exterminated, the assault would continue.

At 3:00 p.m., the battle resumed with a fiery vigor. The Red Sticks lit cotton balls affixed to the end of their arrows and fired them into the fort's wooden structures. The structures, made of longleaf pine, gradually took fire and began to blaze with a white-hot intensity. Coupled with the burning August sun, the stress of battle and the now inaccessible wells, the fort's defenders began to wither.[160] Meanwhile, the dehydrated Red Sticks simply wandered off to the swamps to cool down.

Dixon Bailey and his comrades had no such respite. The battle, the heat, the missiles, the fire, the screams and the fear continued unabated. Perhaps worst of all was the realization that the end was a foregone conclusion: a burning, torturous death at the hands of warriors who despised him and his fellow *métis* more than they did the White invaders of their homeland. Dixon Bailey was a marked man. The Red Sticks were sacrificing dozens of warriors they could not afford to sacrifice to get to him and his fellow *métis*.

Bailey's own sister was captured, and when queried as to her family, she answered honestly and defiantly, pointing at Dixon's brother, James Bailey: "I am the sister of that great man you murdered there." She was immediately thrown down and cut open and her intestines scattered about her. Most of the *métis* women ended up disemboweled as punishment for birthing children and then forcing them to live apart from their Creek heritage.[161]

By now there was very little to fight for. Dixon; his crippled son, Ralph; his slave, Tom; and his friend Dr. Thomas Holmes, along with the latter's slave, made a run for it, trying to reach the woods northeast of the fort. Tom carried the boy, while Dixon and Holmes fired at Red Sticks in pursuit. Dixon was shot mortally, but his slave was able to escape deep into the woods with Ralph. Mercifully, Dixon was dead before it was discovered that Tom later returned to the fort and delivered the boy to the Red Sticks, who promptly dispatched him with a war club.

At five o'clock in the evening, the slaughter ended. Nearly the entire garrison was dead, wounded or captured. The victorious Red Sticks lost close to one hundred warriors, but they had captured a fortified American fort—a rare feat in the annals of Indian warfare.

Settlers throughout the Tensaw region fled their farms upon hearing of the massacre at Fort Mims. The Red Sticks had achieved their objective, but

Fort Mims would be the highpoint of their war against the Americans and traitor-Creeks.

From then on, the Red Sticks—and the Creek Nation as a whole—experienced nothing but calamity. The massacre at Fort Mims galvanized the Americans in a way rarely seen before and not seen again until the modern era. Andrew Jackson, the American Lion, stormed down on the Red Sticks and exacted the revenge his country clamored for. With five hundred Creek and Cherokee allies, Jackson decimated the Red Stick forces at Talladega and Horseshoe Bend, causing the survivors to flee to Florida, where they would attach themselves to the Seminole Nation and continue their war against Jackson and the United States.

Despite the crucial aid rendered by the Lower Creeks, Jackson would later be instrumental in removing all Creeks from their lands, thus turning the Red Stick victory at Fort Mims into the Trail of Tears.[162]

THE AMERICANS

1814, Horseshoe Bend
Davy Crockett

Davy Crockett and his companions approached the Red Stick town, accompanied by a detachment of Cherokees and led by two friendly Creeks. When they reached the town undetected, the allied contingent split in two and followed the two Creeks in opposite circles until the two forces reunited in a cordon around the town, trapping the Red Sticks inside.

A unit of rangers rode toward the houses. The alarmed Red Stick warriors charged the cavalry and pursued them right into the jaws of death. Crockett and his Indian allies opened a devastating fire, sending the Red Sticks back toward their houses. Realizing the hopelessness of resistance, most of the women and some of the warriors threw themselves on the mercy of the Americans. However, forty-six ran toward a house, determined to resist until the end. Crockett watched as a squaw sat at the door and

> *placed her feet against the bow she had in her hand, and then took an arrow, and, raising her feet, she drew with all her might, and let fly at us, and she killed a man, whose name, I believe, was Moore. He was a lieutenant, and his death so enraged us all, that she was fired on, and had at least twenty*

A Captain of the Maroons (1796). *Beinecke Library at Yale University.*

> *balls blown through her. This was the first man I ever saw killed with a*
> *bow and arrow. We now shot them like dogs; and then set the house on fire,*
> *and burned it up with the forty-six warriors in it.*[163]

Crockett then noticed a twelve-year-old boy with a broken thigh and arm lying next to the burning house. As the fire intensified, the boy began to burn and sweat profusely. Still, he would not cry out or ask for quarter, preferring to escape the flames by slowly and quietly and painfully inching away from his burning friends and family.[164]

The victorious Americans led more than one hundred Red Stick prisoners to Fort Strother. The next day, they returned to the scene of the massacre. After killing all inside the house, the fire must have died quickly, for none of the condemned was entirely consumed by the flames. Instead, they were charred— clearly human but in a monstrous state, "a very terrible appearance":

> It was, somehow or other, found out that the house had a potatoe [sic] cellar under it, and an immediate examination was made, for we were all as hungry as wolves. We found a fine chance of potatoes in it, and hunger compelled us to eat them, though I had a little rather not, if I could have helped it, for the oil of the Indians we had burned up on the day before had run down on them, and they looked like they had been stewed with fat meat.[165]

The ravenous Crockett and his companions feasted on the recently cooked potatoes.

After helping rescue an allied Creek fort at Talladega, Crockett returned home to Tennessee:

> I thought they could get along without me for a short time; so I got a furlough and went home, for we had had hard times again on this hunt, and I began to feel as though I had done Indian fighting enough for one time. I remained at home until after the army had returned to the Horseshoe bend, and fought the battle there. But not being with them at that time, of course no history of that fight can be expected of me.[166]

And so, Davy Crockett missed the decisive battle of the Red Stick War in which Andrew Jackson soundly defeated the Creeks' last real chance to defend their ancestral lands. Jackson's 2,700 American soldiers and 600 Cherokee and Creek allies nearly wiped out the Red Stick force of 1,000, with very few casualties of their own. The Red Stick leader, Chief Menawa, took what little remained of his force to continue the resistance with the Seminoles in Florida.

"Soon after [the Battle of Horseshoe Bend], an army was raised to go to Pensacola, and I determined to go again with them, for I wanted a small taste of British fighting, and I supposed they would be there."[167] But

Crockett and his pals arrived too late. General Andrew Jackson had already taken Pensacola from the British (who were forcibly "borrowing" the port and fort from the Spanish).

Crockett's regiment was ordered by Jackson to head southwest "to kill up the Indians on the Scamby river."[168] Along the way, the soldiers spent three days at the ruined Fort Mims, where one of the survivors told his terrifying tale of the massacre and his own narrow escape into the swamps. The survivor then joined Crockett's troop, no doubt hoping to avenge the mother, father, four sisters and four brothers he saw butchered before his eyes. As Crockett later put it, "his tale greatly excited my feelings." As events would soon play out, his tale—and the fate of Fort Mims in general—excited a great many feelings.[169]

Crockett's regiment feasted on the cows that had been wandering the woods and swamps since being scattered during the massacre—a much more palatable meal than the potatoes eaten near Fort Strother—and then continued their hunt.

Once the army arrived at the Escambia River, Crockett and sixteen men were sent across to scout. Choctaw and Chickasaw scouts accompanied him. Along the way, their Indian allies came across two Creeks who were searching for escaped horses. Pretending to be deserters from Jackson's army in Pensacola, the allied scouts smoked and chatted with the two Creek warriors. When the Creeks turned to return to their camp, the Indians immediately shot down one and then ran down the other, killing the Creek with a blow to the head.

When Crockett and his men heard the first shot, they took off running in the direction of the firing. Upon arrival, Crockett saw the two slain Creek warriors lying on the ground, headless:

> [A]nd each of those Indians with us would walk up to one of the heads, and taking his war club would strike on it. This was done by every one of them; and when they had got done, I took one of their clubs, and walked up as they had done, and struck it on the head also. At this they all gathered round me, and patting me on the shoulder, would call me "Warrior—warrior."[170]

Crockett and company continued their hunting of Red Sticks the following morning. Another detachment of enemy Creeks was captured and sent to Fort Montgomery under care of America's Indian allies:

I did hear, that after they left us, the Indians killed and scalped all the prisoners, and I never heard the report contradicted. I cannot positively say it was true, but I think it entirely probable, for it is very much like the Indian character.[171]

And Crockett, his comrades and the inexorable flood of land-hungry Americans continued to roll over the Gulf Coast, claiming empty land and conquering settled land—very much like the American character.

Chapter 10

THE BROTHERS LAFFITE
CHOOSE SIDES, 1814

THE RENEGADES

1814, New Orleans and Barataria
The Brothers Laffite

July 8, 1814
New Orleans

With Louisiana becoming a member of the United States in 1812, support for the Laffites and their associates began to waver. The American authorities began to crack down on lawlessness by land and sea. The "pirate days" of New Orleans were quickly coming to a close.

In 1813, the Laffite brothers were charged with violating the U.S. revenue laws. As proof that many in New Orleans still embraced the smugglers, the charges went unenforced. The brothers, and Pierre in particular, continued to make frequent visits to the city, both for business and the pleasure of visiting his *placee* mistress, Marie Villard, at their house on Dumaine Street. The continued presence of the Laffites in New Orleans, coupled with the embarrassment the base at Grand Terre caused the American administration, led to a raid on the Villard house on July 8, 1814. A surprised Pierre was escorted to the prison behind the Cabildo, off the Place d'Armes.[172]

September 3, 1814
Grand Terre and Grand Isle

Jean watched as a warship approached his Baratarian base. His curiosity was piqued when he saw the ship fire on a boat leaving Grand Terre but then drop anchor and wait. And wait some more.

Jean boarded a pirogue and rowed out to meet the puzzling ship. Too late did he recognize the British flag. Fortunately for Jean, the British soldiers did not recognize him and claimed to be carrying a packet of letters for the pirate chief. Jean escorted them to shore, and only then did he reveal himself. The British officer had been telling the truth. Rather than looking to arrest Jean, he hoped to woo him. His Royal Majesty had an offer for the chief of Barataria.

Laffite was offered pardon for his and his men's recent attacks on British ships, as well as extensive land grants once Britain defeated the Americans. Jean himself was offered a captaincy in the British army. In exchange, he and his followers would serve in the British army and surrender their Batatarian fleet to the British commander.

Jean thanked the officer for his proposal and asked for fifteen days to make a decision, implying that he needed time to convince his followers to come along with him. Jean's request was only to buy time. He already knew where his loyalties lay: to himself and Pierre.

Accepting the British offer would be of little benefit. Land was cheap, a captain's pay negligible and life under British rule unprofitable, for Britain vigorously prosecuted pirates and was currently entertaining the idea of an empire-wide ban on slavery, the Laffites' cash cow. On the other hand, the United States had even less to offer the Laffites. America, too, would crack down on piracy and smuggling should the nation emerge victorious. But unlike Britain, the United States would continue to embrace the peculiar institution that had enriched the Laffites. Regardless of the war's outcome, the brothers had already determined to relocate somewhere off the Mexican coast. Yet good relations with American merchants, middlemen and slave owners would be essential to their success.

Jean promptly dispatched the British packet of letters to authorities in New Orleans.[173]

September 4, 1814

Pierre's cell was opened. The elder Laffite emerged a free man, freed three slaves on his way out and made his way to Jean at Grand Terre. The brothers Laffite were soon to be reunited. They would orchestrate one of their biggest sales to date and then use the earnings to reestablish themselves away from prying American eyes.[174]

September 15, 1814
Grand Terre

It was to be a big day at Grand Terre. The Laffite brothers stood to make a small fortune. A week before, the privateer *Moon of November* arrived loaded with the goods of a recently captured Spanish merchantman, most notably wine and rum. The ever-trustworthy Dominique You had arrived. Vincent Gambi and other notable pirates had arrived from Mexico. A privateer from Cartagena was docked and awaiting repairs along with several other ships. In fact, a veritable fleet of confederated pirates, privateers and smugglers lay anchored or beached at the Laffite base. Even better, merchant boats and pirogues were arriving by the hour from New Orleans.

Yes, tomorrow was going to be a big day. A big, profitable day. The biggest sale in recent memory.[175]

Four Days Prior
New Orleans

At one o'clock in the morning, seventy men boarded three barges and set sail in the direction of Grand Terre. They soon rendezvoused with Commodore Patterson's fleet, which included the *Carolina*, *Seahorse* and six gunboats. By September 15, everything was in place. In the morning, they would rid the Baratarian swamps of the "hellish banditti."[176]

September 15, 1814
Grand Terre

Jean's connections in New Orleans no doubt alerted him to the impending raid. He seems not to have been overly concerned. After all, he had just recently alerted Governor Claiborne to the British menace and handed over verifying documentation. He had cast his die with the Americans. Surely, they would not harass him now?

Several captains urged Jean to flee with them to Cartagena before the Americans blocked their escape. Jean calculated the odds. There were four hundred men on the island, but most were sailors, not soldiers. They had signed on as privateers expecting to prey on unarmed merchantmen and flee from warships. Rarely did a privateer or pirate give battle. Neither could he count on his customers to take up arms against the United States. True, he had plenty of ships, but most were smaller craft better designed for smuggling and navigating the bayous of Barataria. Other boats were docked or beached while being repaired. He had three cannons, but they were mounted on logs instead of carriages and would be heavily outgunned by the approaching fleet.

Still, the goods were here, the buyers were here and the U.S. fleet was not here…yet. The gambler made his decision. The sale would go on. The houses on Grand Terre opened for business, and the merchandise was spread along the beach. Jean would see the sales through and then flee.

The only precaution he took was to hide gunpowder and flints inland. It would be the only good decision Jean made that day.[177]

September 16, 1814
Grand Terre

At 8:30 a.m., Patterson's fleet appeared on the horizon, sooner than Jean had hoped. Pandemonium ensued. The merchants and buyers leaped into their small craft, hoping to reach the mainland ahead of the fleet. The Cartagena privateers formed a line of battle, prepared to fight their way out. Jean and Pierre boarded a pirogue and made for the German Coast.

For an hour and a half, tension and chaos filled the air. Finally, at 10:00 a.m. Patterson attacked. Because Jean had allowed each man and ship to decide its own fate, there was no concerted response to the American raid. Some privateers immediately surrendered. Others tried unsuccessfully to escape. Still others began to burn their ships and prizes.

It was all to no avail. Within two hours, Patterson had captured the "Baratarian fleet." Pirogues were fleeing in all directions. The brothers' most trusted comrade, Dominique You, was among the captured.

Then the plundering and destruction began. Patterson's men gathered and secured the merchandise still spread across the beach. They ransacked the

Soldier or Pirate at Ruin, by Bernardus Theodorus van Loo (1844). *Rijksmuseum.*

forty houses before burning them, along with the watchtowers, warehouses and any boat deemed unseaworthy or not worth the tote back to New Orleans. Those ships that were still seaworthy—and that would fetch a good price at auction—were added to Patterson's fleet.

The haul was astounding. Between captured ships, loot, cannons and hard cash, Patterson sailed into New Orleans with $250,000 worth of goods (or about $6 million in 2023).[178] It was a crushing blow to the Laffite operation.

The reaction in New Orleans was predictably mixed. Honest merchants and those with no stake in the smuggling racket were pleased that law and order would reign in New Orleans, that everyone would receive a fair shake. Just as many were aghast at the raid, for Patterson brought back with him numerous incriminating documents tying respected New Orleans merchants to the Laffites.

As dramatic as the Barataria raid had been, it was soon forgotten as more urgent news reached the city: the British were coming.[179]

December 1814
New Orleans

Through intermediaries, Jean contacted General Andrew Jackson with his own offer: back on smoldering Grand Isle, back on the base the Americans had destroyed, lay buried in the sand a pirate treasure, desperately needed by the American forces: 7,500 flints.[180]

Chapter 11

THE BATTLE OF NEW ORLEANS, 1815

THE BRITISH

1814–1815, New Orleans
George Robert Gleig

February 1815
Dauphin Island

The lieutenant reached down and quietly lifted a fir apple potato in his left hand.[181] He waited in ambush, crouched behind the dune, as his enemy approached. Seven of his comrades had already fallen. He was determined not to be the eighth.

Closer the enemy came. Closer still. The officer lay down in the sand, clutching the only weapon he had, and prayed that the warrior would pass him by. He did. The lieutenant quietly arose, took aim and hurled his death-dart.

"Damn you, you poltroon!" shouted the soldier whose cheek now bore the mark of the dreaded spud. The lieutenant let out a whoop and began to run to his side of camp announcing another score for the 85th Infantry.

Later that night, the officers of the 85th, 93rd and 95th Regiments would recount their heroic exploits of the afternoon. Likewise, their enemies of the 7th, 43rd and 14th Dragoons would boast of their own martial achievements.

G.R. Gleig. *New York Public Library*.

One participant, Lieutenant George Robert Gleig, would later recall:

For the space of some days they pelted each other from morning till night, laying ambuscades and exhibiting, on a small scale, all the stratagems of war; whilst the whole army, not even excepting the Generals themselves, stood by and spurred them on.[182]

As the officers of His Britannic Majesty's army dined, lounged and bantered, nearly four hundred of their comrades lay buried in a swampy field, 150 miles to the west.[183]

1814
Port Royal, Jamaica

In 1813, a young Scottish divinity student named George Robert Gleig joined the Duke of Wellington's army as an ensign in the 85th Infantry. Once Napoleon was vanquished, Gleig and his regiment were sent to humble the upstart Americans across the sea. What promised to be a long, illustrious military career was quickly off to an auspicious start. Not only did the eighteen-year-old help send Napoleon into exile, but he was also present when the Americans were crushed at the Battle of Bladensburg and the burning of Washington, D.C. Near the end of 1814, the 85th was sent on yet another campaign—one that would open a third and decisive theater of the War of 1812.

Gleig's regiment was sent south to Jamaica, where it would join an amply sized and supplied army that would sail on a secret mission to New Orleans. The capture of the Crescent City would provide the British with a Gulf base to help secure their Caribbean colonies, as well as provide the southern terminus of a resurgent American empire, linking British Canada to the Gulf of Mexico. With their reliance on the Mississippi River, the Kentucky and the Ohio Valley would then cast their lot with the British (just as the Spanish had hoped a decade before when flirting with Aaron Burr and William Augustus Bowles).[184] And then there was the plunder—the "beauty and booty"—of exotic New Orleans.

No doubt George Gleig and his companions boarded the New Orleans–bound ships full of excitement and expectation.

The Landing
December 22
Ten Miles South of New Orleans

George Robert Gleig, along with 1,600 British soldiers—about one-third of the army—piled into transports and began an eighty-mile journey over frigid, turbulent water to a landing about ten miles south of New Orleans. The sky was dark and foreboding. Soon it began to rain heavily, and when the rain stopped, a frost descended on the luckless soldiers. Cold, unable to move and rocked by the rolling waves, Gleig lost feeling in his arms and legs. And still the journey continued. As night began to set, the charcoal fires burning at the front of each boat were extinguished, making the trip even more frigid and uncomfortable.

As midnight approached, the flotilla threw out its anchors. An American picket was spotted. Should they see the Redcoats, the element of surprise would be lost. A pair of boats were sent to surround and silence the picket. Meanwhile, Gleig and his companions waited in the cold, numb and miserable. When it was ascertained that the picket was taken, the flotilla continued. But the wind that had been pushing them silently along now ceased to blow. It would be necessary to finish the odyssey with oars. Finally, as dawn arose, the lead transport reached its destination, only to be confronted with seven-foot-tall cane rising out of the marsh. Again Gleig and most of the crew waited in their boats as engineers spent two hours clearing a path to solid ground.

At last, Gleig was able to stand up, stiff, sore and nearly frozen. Once his blood began circulating enough to walk, he stepped across his boat into the one in front of him. And then the next and the next, following the single-file line of boats until he stepped out into the swamp water. By nine o'clock in the morning, what seemed an eternity since they began their trek, the British were on dry land, only a brisk march from the gates of New Orleans. And they had made the trip undetected.[185]

The British had pulled off a stunning accomplishment. Of all the roads to New Orleans, they had landed on the one road where surprise was possible. By overcoming the lax sentinels the night before, they had placed themselves in a position to take the city by the end of the day. To be sure, Gleig and his companions would lay low in the marsh until the boats could return with the remaining two-thirds of the army.

Meanwhile, Gleig and the advance force would wait:

> *The place where we landed was as wild as it is possible to imagine. Gaze where we might, nothing could be seen except one huge marsh covered with tall reeds; not a house nor a vestige of human industry could be discovered; and even of trees there were but a few growing upon the banks of the creek. Yet it was such a spot as, above others, favoured our operations. No eye could watch us, or report our arrival to the American General. By remaining quietly among the reeds, we might effectually conceal ourself from notice; because, from appearance all around, it was easy to perceive that the place which we occupied had been seldom, if ever before, marked with a human footstep.*[186]

Rather than wait for reinforcements, the British commander Major General John Keane, convinced that the Americans numbered fewer than five thousand and were scattered throughout the myriad approaches to the city, decided to advance on New Orleans. His advance guard quickly took the first plantation they came to, placing the owner and his brother under arrest. The British were now in control of the river road, only a few hours' march from New Orleans.

Unfortunately for Gleig and his colleagues, the arrested Major Gabriel Villere jumped out a window, onto the balcony and to the yard below. Before the British guard registered what was happening, Villere had put some distance between himself and his captors, disappearing into the tall cane. He ran toward a cluster of cypress trees, but the family hound followed him, threatening to reveal his position. Villere had no choice but to grab a branch and club his loyal dog to death. After a brief search, the British guard returned to the plantation, and Villere descended a tree and crept along the edge of the swamp until he reached a neighboring plantation and spread the alarm: "The British are here!"[187]

The Night Attack
December 23, 1814

With the swamps on their right and the Mississippi River on their left, the British troops marched closer to New Orleans until they were told to halt around noon. Finally, Gleig and comrades were given the chance to rest as comfortably as possible. They were even allowed to light fires so long as they kept their arms nearby. Scant provisions were provided, but meals were supplemented with food from the nearby plantation house and slave quarters. For three hours, the British soldiers lay about, dining, resting and bathing. (The mercurial New Orleans weather had turned uncomfortably warm after the frigid nighttime sail.)

Around three o'clock in the afternoon, bugles sounded from the British pickets, followed by sporadic musket fire. Gleig and company formed ranks, only to be told that the alarm was much ado about nothing—some American cavalry attempted to scout the field but had been driven away.

No doubt the Americans now knew of General Keane's presence. But why worry? American infantry was not likely to challenge His Majesty's troops, the vanquishers of Napoleon, in open battle. Gleig and companions returned to their leisure.

Later that night, around 7:30 p.m., a mysterious ship sailed up the Mississippi, parallel to the British camp. Gleig thought it might be an HMS vessel sent to aid in the capture of the Crescent City. Soldiers ashore hailed the sailors aboard but received no reply. The camp was alerted, and several musket shots were fired in the ship's direction. Silence. And then the vessel began to shift, turning its cannons on the British camp. "Give them this for the honor of America!" Flames erupted from the broadside of the boat as

Andrew Jackson, by Samuel Lovett Waldo (1819). *Metropolitan Museum of Art.*

grapeshot rained down on the British camp. With no cannons capable of returning adequate fire, Gleig and his mates

> *were commanded to leave the fires, and to hasten under the dyke. Thither all accordingly repaired, without much regard to order and regularity, and laying ourselves along wherever we could find room, we listened in painful silence to the pattering of grapeshot among our huts, and to the shrieks and groans of those who lay wounded beside them.*[188]

Andrew Jackson, the American Lion, was stirring.

GLEIG LAY HUDDLED AGAINST the levee. Clouds covered the moon as the embers sputtered around the campfires. Only the blaze from the cannons on the American schooner *Carolina* lit the air. Unable to return fire, the British pressed against the wet ground, praying for succor.

Those prayers went unanswered when musket balls joined the grapeshot in penetrating the British line. At first, Gleig was hopeful that British pickets were either firing at the *Carolina* or were firing panicked rounds at trees in front of them. Then reality set in:

> But these doubts were not permitted to continue long in existence. The dropping fire having paused for a few moments, was succeeded by a fearful yell; and the heavens were illuminated on all sides by a semi-circular blaze of musketry. It was now manifest that we were surrounded, and that by a very superior force; and that no alternative remained, except to surrender at discretion, or to beat back the assailants.[189]

Gleig and his comrades arose to meet the foe. Soon his unit ran into a line of men. Too dark to see, Gleig's closest friend in the army, Captain Charles Grey, supposed the mystery soldiers in front of them to be British, but Gleig had his doubts. Gleig called to the men now aligned against them. No answer. And then came an eruption of musket fire. Believing himself to be the victim of friendly fire, Grey refused to shoot back as his men fell by ones and twos before taking cover. Gleig urged Grey to fire back, but still refusing to believe the Americans had come so close, Grey demurred. He did, however, agree to remain behind a mound as Gleig crawled forward to confirm the identity of the troops just ahead. It *was* the Americans. Grey refused to accept Gleig's report, and the two friends reached a compromise:

> Grey with one half of the party should remain where he was, whilst I with the other half should make a short detour to the right, and come down upon the flank of the line from whose fire we had suffered so severely. The plan was carried into immediate execution. Taking with me about a dozen or fourteen men, I quitted Grey, and we never met again.[190]

Gleig took little satisfaction in being right. For the next seven hours, from eight in the evening until three in the morning, British and American soldiers waged a desperate and bloody hand-to-hand battle. Should American forces triumph, the British would be driven back into the Gulf, their army annihilated. Should Britain win and advance, New Orleans lay naked, with

Jackson having wagered everything on a risky night assault. Both sides fought like Furies, knowing the consequences.

Campfire, musket fire, cannon fire; hacking, slashing, parrying, thrusting; swinging, kicking, biting; shouting, threatening, pleading, moaning (in English, always in English); deception, friendly fire, confusion; darkness, chaos, terror; exhaustion, adrenaline, exhilaration; life, pain, unconsciousness and death.

Gleig stood amid battle, exhausted but exhilarated with victory. The Americans had been driven back. His Majesty's forces had withstood a surprise attack at night. Flushed with victory, Gleig stood with two swords in his hand—his own and a surrendered American sword—as the bugles sounded the American retreat. Then an officer stepped forward and dampened Gleig's mood:

> It came upon me like a thunderbolt; and casting aside my trophy, thought only of the loss which I had sustained. Regardless of every other matter I ran to the rear, and found Grey lying behind the dung-heap, motionless and cold. A little pool of blood which had coagulated under his head, pointed out the spot where the ball had entered, and the position of his limbs gave proof that he must have died without a struggle. I cannot pretend to describe what were then my sensations, but whatever nature they might be, little time was given for their indulgence; the bugle sounding the alarm, I was compelled to leave him as he lay, and to join my corps.[191]

Flushed with battle and survival but shocked and distraught over the death of his friend, Gleig lay on the ground in stunned silence. The *Carolina* continued to launch shells into the British camp. Cold, exhausted and hungry, Gleig arose and went with two comrades to retrieve his friend's corpse. No stranger to the mangled flesh of war, Gleig was horrified by what he saw on the field of battle:

> A man shot through the head or heart lies as if he were in a deep slumber; insomuch that when you gaze upon him you experience little else than pity. But of these, many had met their deaths from bayonet wounds, sabre cuts, or heavy blows from the butt end of muskets; and the consequence was, that not only were the wounds themselves exceedingly frightful, but the very countenances of the dead exhibited the most savage and ghastly expressions. Friends and foes lay together in small groups of four or six, nor was it difficult to tell almost the very hand by which some of them had fallen. Nay,

such had been the deadly closeness of the strife, that in one or two places an English and American soldier might be seen with the bayonet of each fastened in the other's body.[192]

Gleig finally found his friend's body. With the fighting over, reality set in: Charles was dead. Gleig broke down weeping beside his friend's body. After spilling his tears and gathering himself, he placed Grey's corpse in a cart and took him to the field hospital, where he buried him in the garden. "I laid him there as a soldier should be laid, arrayed, not in a shroud, but in his uniform."[193] Gleig's grief and devotion to his friend caused the two privates helping him to also shed tears. Too many soldiers had died that night. Some of those who survived wished they hadn't.

After burying his friend, Gleig walked through the hospital: "It is here that war loses is grandeur and show, and presents only a real picture of its effects."[194] The room was crowded with all sorts of wounded—the unconscious, the recently dead, those in agony, those being amputated, the already amputated, the screaming, the insensible and the dead. And then he walked into the officers' room and froze in horror. Here were his associates, his friends, the officers he knew on a personal level:

> But there was one among the rest whose appearance was too horrible ever to be forgotten. He had been shot through the windpipe, and the breath making its way between the skin and the flesh had dilated him to a size absolutely terrific. His head and face were particularly shocking. Every feature was enlarged beyond what can well be imagined; whilst his eyes were so completely hidden by the cheeks and forehead as to destroy all resemblance to a human countenance.[195]

Gleig could not yet know that the horrors of the night battle and the hospital were only a harbinger of evils to come.

Reconnaissance
December 28

After leaving the field of battle to the British in the early morning hours of December 24, General Jackson stationed his men behind the Rodriguez Canal—two miles from the British and six from New Orleans—and immediately began to strengthen his position. Jackson made the Macarty house his headquarters and ordered his men to dig, to keep digging and then to dig some more. Knowing that the British were expecting reinforcements and that they must march through him to take New Orleans, Jackson intended to construct an insurmountable breastwork.

Racing against time, the Americans dug in. By Christmas Day, they had a strong breastwork, fitted out with cannons, some manned by Dominique You and the recently pardoned Baratarians. Other celebrities joined Jackson's army, including two of the Kemper brothers, a contingent of Choctaws under Pushmataha and a unit of free persons of color. The *Carolina* and *Louisiana* protected their left flank, while the swamp secured their right. One of Jackson's men, Pierre Laffite, urged the general to extend his left flank into the swamps to prevent a British flanking maneuver. Laffite's request would turn the tide of battle.

As the Americans strengthened their position, the British were rejoicing at the arrival of General Edward Pakenham. Pakenham was the brother-in-law of the nearly deified Duke of Wellington. Now the soldiers who had defeated Napoleon would be led by Wellington's kin. Victory was certain.

The American frigate *Chesapeake* approaches the British ship *Shannon* in this painting by R. Dodd (1813). *Smithsonian Libraries.*

Pakenham furthered buoyed his troops by sinking the *Carolina* and forcing the *Louisiana* to flee to the safety of the American line. The ships that had harassed the British 24/7 for nearly a week were now silenced. The next day, December 28, Pakenham ordered his men to assemble and march toward Jackson's defensive line. His primary goal was knowledge—to test and seek out a weakness in the American line. If he found a weakness that could be immediately exploited, he would order a full-scale assault. If not, he would retire with a better understanding of the American defenses—knowledge that he would use to formulate the battle plan that would ensure the sack of New Orleans.

On a frigid, frosty morning, those who sent Napoleon into exile marched on Jackson's line. Congreve rockets fired over their head, and British cannonballs crashed into the American position. Bugles and drums urged His Majesty's troops on. Closer and closer they came to the American breastwork, which now reached five feet high with cannons protruding through. Jackson's line was impromptu and incomplete but quite formidable. Soon, the men behind that line would demonstrate exactly how formidable.

Cannons exploded, and shells and balls screamed toward the oncoming British troops from the American line to the front and from the *Louisiana* on their left flank. Lieutenant Gleig was stunned by the ferocity and accuracy of the American response: "Scarce a bullet passed over, or fell short of its mark, but all striking full into the midst of our ranks, occasioned terrible havoc."[196]

If there was a weakness in the American line, Pakenham did not find it on December 28. Instead, he ordered the men on his left to take what shelter they could. American marksmanship forced Gleig and his fellow light infantry to hug the damp ground and wait for nightfall, when they could quietly sulk back to their camp two miles away. The Battle for New Orleans had ground to an embarrassing halt.

Pakenham knew that he had to act and soon; his troops were growing demoralized. And yet the Americans had shown little weakness. True, their left flank (the British right) had been outnumbered, and if it weren't for the disaster near the river, the British might have overrun the swamp flank. But Jackson quickly rectified that weakness. In addition, he continued to improve his embankment and brought his number of cannons up to thirteen. Unless Pakenham's own artillery could reduce the fortification or disable the American cannons, a frontal assault would prove disastrous.

On New Year's Eve, Pakenham's men silently marched to within six hundred yards of Jackson's line. They quietly built up their own earthworks and laboriously dragged their own cannons into place. They were aided by a dense fog that rolled in at dawn, protecting them from American fire. Finally, at eight o'clock in the morning, the fog lifted and thunder boomed as Pakenham's twenty-two guns began to belch balls and shells and rockets toward Jackson's defenses. Unfortunately, their lower elevation caused many of the projectiles to fly harmlessly over the Americans. One shot, however, landed on a powder carriage and caused a terrific explosion. Gleig and his fellow soldiers erupted in cheers. A few more accurate shots later, and with enough American cannons silenced, the infantry would storm the breach.

Again, Pakenham amassed his troops into two columns, one opposing the American right and the other the left. He only needed his artillery to create the breach.

It didn't. By midafternoon, Pakenham had recognized the futility of his artillery duel. He had managed to silence some American cannons, but he had suffered more damage himself. Worse, his artillery failed to damage the American breastwork. Pakenham ordered another retreat. A discouraged Gleig related, "We retired, therefore, not only baffled and disappointed, but in some degree disheartened and discontented. All our plans had as yet proved abortive."[197]

Battle
January 8

Pakenham knew by now that only two options remained to him: retreat or an immediate, all-out, winner-take-all assault on Jackson's line. Dysentery was ravaging his camp. His food supplies were running low and of increasingly poor quality. American snipers were disrupting sleep. Most importantly, his men were growing more restless and discouraged by the day. Soldiers like Gleig were tired of the cannonade and sharpshooters and eager for a fight: "They resembled rather the growling of a chained dog, when he sees his adversary and cannot reach him; for in all their complaints, no man ever hinted at a retreat, whilst all were eager to bring matters to the issue of a battle, at any sacrifice of loves."[198]

A desperate Pakenham decided to roll the die: he would attack Jackson's line and then sack New Orleans on January 8.

Two additional regiments arrived on January 6, giving Pakenham more than 8,000 soldiers to dislodge the Americans. The British general concocted a battle plan whereby 1,400 of his men, including Gleig's 85th under Colonel William Thornton, would cross the Mississippi River, storm the battery Jackson had erected on his right flank and turn those cannons on the Americans. The latter would then be caught in a crossfire between the now-British guns on their right and British guns to their immediate front. The Americans would be forced to leave their daunting fortifications and then easily be dispersed by the more disciplined British. All Pakenham need do was wait for his own left flank to rout the far American right across the river and fire a signal rocket into the air. Pakenham, Gleig and company would then finish the mop-up operation and retrieve the booty of New Orleans.[199]

And then Murphy's law struck the British army. Only 350 soldiers of the left flank made it to the opposite shore.[200] Worse, they landed eight hours behind schedule. Not only had they lost the element of surprise, but their chances of taking the American flank by force were also greatly diminished. Pakenham declared to an aide, "Thornton's people will be of no use whatever to the general attack." When another aide suggested delaying the attack and retreating before the sun came up, the proud but resigned general replied, "I have twice deferred the attack. We are strong in numbers now comparatively. It will cost more men, [but] the assault must be made.… Smith, order the rocket to be fired."[201]

Death of Pakenham at the Battle of New Orleans, by W. Ridgway (1860). *Library of Congress.*

Andrew Jackson at the Battle of New Orleans, by Ethel Magafan (1943). *Library of Congress.*

With that decision, the fate of 2,434 soldiers was decided. On the British left flank, Gleig's 85th Regiment, much delayed by the river crossing, marched toward the American right. Meanwhile, the main assault began to materialize in front of Line Jackson.

Gleig glumly looked over his boat and noticed the muffled oars. All around him was silence. Every conceivable precaution had been taken to ensure the element of surprise. And then Gleig looked up to the sky, where the sun was beginning to rise. Fog covered the field, but daylight was upon them. They were still four miles from the American batteries. The batteries should have been taken an hour before. And worst of all, Gleig heard a loud *crack* and *whoosh* and looked to his right. The signal rocket was screeching into the dawn's early light.

Thornton and his 350 men marched on. Within half an hour, they arrived at an American outpost and stormed it at the double-quick. The Americans fled. Gleig and comrades advanced toward the main line, where another large American force awaited them.

Thornton spread his men across the American defenses and stormed the positions. The Americans discharged their cannons and followed quickly with a fusillade of musketry. Three Brits fell dead, with another forty wounded. Still, they advanced, fired and then stormed the line, descending the ditch in front and then ascending the wall above. The Americans fled. The 85th pursued. Word began to spread that their comrades on the right of the river were experiencing similar success. The pursuit continued.

Two miles later, another messenger arrived with sobering news: the main assault had stalled. Worse, it had been an utter failure. The Americans' left flank had held (thanks to Pierre Laffite's urging that the line be extended deeper into the swamp). The frontal assault had failed on account of the accuracy of American cannons (including the pardoned Baratarians), but mostly because the British 44th Regiment had failed to bring forth the scaling ladders, without which the soldiers were unable to ascend the high walls of the American rampart. Sitting ducks, those who made it to the walls after enduring a blistering hail of cannonballs were mowed down by concealed Americans on the defenses above. Now all three columns of the main attack were in retreat. The day was lost. The 85th was ordered to fall back.

Gleig was charged with establishing a rear guard at a nearby chateau. While the remainder of Thornton's force retraced its steps, Gleig's unit covered its retreat. When the Americans, emboldened by the total victory across the river, began to reconnoiter, Gleig had to act fast. He feigned an advance on the Americans, causing them to return to their line. Gleig then burned the chateau and, under the cover of smoke, rejoined the rest of Thornton's men, who were now rowing across the river.[202]

Rowing back across the Mississippi River, Gleig understood that His Majesty's forces had been crushed and humiliated. What he could not prepare for was the extent of the destruction and totality of defeat that awaited him across the river.

Retreat
January 9–26, 1815

Of the 10,000 fellow comrades-in-arms Gleig had marched with in hopes of "beauty and booty," 300 would never march again. Another 1,500 would carry their wounds—some sooner, some later—with them to the next world. The field below Jackson's Line ran, at least metaphorically, with blood, the actual blood of 2,000 casualties sinking into the soft mud that they had furtively traversed, back and forth, back and forth, over the past month. There was no doubt about it: the attack on New Orleans had been an unmitigated disaster. Gleig wrote home to his sister that "it has been a bloody business."[203]

Still, some hoped to regroup and try again. Most prayed that their leaders would see the inevitable. That is, what leaders remained, for Pakenham had died on the field of glory, with Gibbs writhing in pain next to him and soon to join his general in death. Keane, too, was shot out of action.[204] The present powers that be finally ordered a general withdrawal.

Fearful that an empowered Jackson would leave his line to turn a British defeat into an annihilation, the British retreated back through the marshes and into the safety of the Gulf methodically, with the last units leaving the coast on January 26, two and a half weeks after the disastrous January 8 assault.

Once safely aboard a British ship, Gleig learned that his friend Charles Grey had bequeathed to him his pistols, books and dog.[205]

The Fir Apple War
February, 1815, Dauphin Island

The fir apple war raged on. So many had fallen to more lethal projectiles in the previous months that a bruise from the dreaded spud was a welcome diversion from the recent memories that haunted the island's transient inhabitants.

Each evening, ensign Gleig retired to his tent with bruises on his body and ghosts in his mind:

> [Charles Grey] *was as brave a soldier and as good a man as the British army can boast of; beloved by his brother officers and adored by his men. To me he was as a brother; nor have I ceased even now to feel, as often as the 23rd of December returns, that on that night a tie was broken than which the progress of human life will hardly furnish more tender or more strong.*[206]

Gleig and what was left of his companions were forced to wait on the island until a frigate returned to escort them back to England. They waited. And waited. And waited. Boredom—the eternal curse of the soldier.

Spring began to give way to summer. Snakes began to infest the camp. Dormant alligators began to move. The snakes and alligators quickly became acclimated to the presence of men. One afternoon, two camp followers, a woman and her child, entered their tent to find a curious—and thankfully not too hungry—alligator lounging in the shade.[207]

Finally, in March 1815, Gleig was able to board the ship that would take him home, the war finally over. With inexpressible joy, his transport approached the coast of England. And then lightning struck his soul: Napoleon had escaped. Europe, once again, would be engulfed in war. Win or lose, Gleig and his colleagues were doomed to relive the horrors of battle.

Chapter 12

MANIFEST DESTINY, 1816–1835

THE BLACKS

1816, Negro Fort, Apalachicola River, Spanish Territory
Garcon

In the spring of 1815, Lieutenant George Robert Gleig, fresh off his New Orleans defeat and potato war victory, arrived at a village near Apalachicola Bay. Strangely, it was occupied by a band of Choctaw Indians and "consisted of upwards of thirty huts, composed of reeds and branches of trees, erected in the heart of a wood, without any regard to form or regularity." One hundred Choctaw warriors lounged around, their women hard at work. If the ever-perceptive Gleig had been aware of Gulf Coast Indian-British relations, he would have immediately recognized the oddity of Choctaw Indians trading with (and later laying down their lives in defense of) a British turned ex-slave fort. Most Choctaws had cast their lot with the Americans. Choctaw warriors had just helped defeat both the British at New Orleans and the Creeks in Alabama. And yet here they were, defending one of the most unique fortifications in the entire United States.[208]

Negro Fort had been built by British soldiers atop an old Panton, Leslie & Company trading post at Prospect Bluff.[209] Upon the British evacuation of the Gulf Coast following the disaster at New Orleans, the British handed the fort, its uniforms and war materiel over to the runaway slaves they had been actively recruiting. A number of these former slaves had served in the Colonial Marines. While many people of color had elected to evacuate with British forces to the Caribbean, a large number decided to remain on the continent. They were now led by three valuable former slaves from Pensacola: Cyrus, a twenty-six-year-old "mulatto" carpenter and cooper; Prince, a twenty-six-year-old carpenter and lieutenant in the Colonial Marines; and, most notably, Garcon, the "French Negro," a thirty-year-old carpenter and master sergeant.[210]

While the fortification was professional and impressive, a Maroon colony inside slaveholding Spanish territory, and on the border of an ever-expanding United States, stood little chance of survival. However, good relations with local Indians and a constant supply of reinforcements enabled the fort and community to prosper. Trade with the Seminoles was vital and also easily accessible, for the Seminoles also distrusted and feared American encroachment on their lands. Other Black freedmen and runaway slaves flocked to the fort. A Black Spanish deserter arrived from St. Augustine with thirty to forty runaways. British captain George Woodbine brought seventy more escaped slaves from East Florida. Many more slaves arrived from the United States, including some who had escaped from the plantation of Indian agent Benjamin Hawkins, who had helped capture William Augustus Bowles a decade before.[211]

The self-sustainability of a runaway slave Maroon colony was not an acceptable reality to the new United States. General Andrew Jackson was especially incensed. Most southerners—and Americans in general, including President James Monroe—soon came around to Jackson's way of thinking, as more and more slaves fled their masters and made their way to Negro Fort.

Emboldened by their increasing numbers, the soldiers of Negro Fort added a small navy to their arsenal by stealing or constructing more than a dozen schooners, barks and canoes (including one forty-five feet long). Two of the boats were armed with cannons, and the pirates began raiding vessels on the lower Apalachicola River. The Maroon pirates established a base at Dog Island at the entrance to the Apalachicola and allied with other local pirates to raid all non-English ships. Pensacola merchant John Innerarity, an Englishman living in Spanish Pensacola with connections to Panton, Leslie & Company, complained, "They are now organized as Pirates, have several small Vessels well armed, & some Piracies that lately occurred in the Lakes are supposed to have been committed by them."[212]

Jackson ordered General Edmund Gaines to eradicate the Maroon fort and community. He wrote to the U.S. secretary of war that American forces will soon have "attended to the subject of this negroe fort and put an end to the lawless Depredations of this Banditti of *Land Pirates*."[213]

Determined to do his part, Indian agent Hawkins appealed to those Seminoles and Creeks with whom he still had influence. More concerned with recovering valuable runaway slaves than destroying a self-sustained Maroon fortress, Hawkins promised his Indian allies fifty dollars for each runaway they returned. (He even asked Governor Zuniga to offer a similar bounty and reminded him that America had helped Spain get rid of William Augustus Bowles a decade before.)[214] Hawkins further sweetened the deal—albeit with a veiled threat—by suggesting that if Creeks captured and returned runaway slaves, "Their masters will stay at home and be peaceable and friendly and your paths of peace and trade will be free and open."[215] The Indian agent then reported, "[Indians were] making an effort of themselves to aid the Seminole Chiefs in destroying the negro establishments in that country, and capturing and delivering all Negros belonging to Citizens of the United States, to me, or to some of our military establishments."[216]

On July 10, 1816, four U.S. gunboats from New Orleans and Bay St. Louis arrived at the Apalachicola River carrying 50 sailors, provisions and cannons. At the same time, an American force of 116 soldiers from Camp Crawford in southwest Georgia headed south, where they rendezvoused with 150 Lower Creek warriors under William McIntosh and, later, another unit of Creek warriors. All Indians had been promised fifty dollars for each slave they returned to U.S. custody. To ensure their loyalty, the United States had also promised them that they could keep anything they could carry from Negro Fort, excepting cannons and arms.

On July 16, a U.S. gunboat noticed a small craft near the shore. An American officer dropped and boarded a small boat and sailed over to investigate. As he near the suspicious craft, the enemy fired on him. The Americans retaliated, and the smaller, faster craft fled. The Battle of Negro Fort had begun.[217]

Two days later, a U.S. boat carrying four sailors and an officer, searching for fresh water, noticed a Black man standing alone on the shore. They sailed over to ascertain the identity of the loiterer. As soon as the Americans disembarked, two columns of twenty warriors each, led by Garcon and a Choctaw, emerged from their ambush, firing on the unsuspecting sailors. Three died instantly. One sailor dove into the water and swam to safety. The fifth was captured and taken to Negro Fort, where he was tarred and burnt alive. A few days later, a Black warrior from Negro Fort was captured carrying the scalp of the burnt man to Seminole allies.[218]

Only July 20, American forces and their Indian allies surrounded the fort. Unwilling to challenge the arsenal inside the fort, for six days the American army waited in the background, allowing the Creek warriors the "opportunity" to recover as many slaves as possible and therefore earn their fifty dollars per head. The two sides exchanged sporadic musket fire, along with a barrage of cannonballs fired from the fort. Then the Blacks, many outfitted in British uniforms, sortied from the fort. Hand-to-hand combat ensued. Still the Americans remained in the background with the goal of minimizing casualties.

Eventually, the Blacks retreated to their fort. Chief McIntosh sent a delegation under a flag of truce to the fort. Garcon replied that "he had been left by British Government and…would sink any American vessels that should attempt to pass it, and would blow up the Fort if he could not defend it."[219]

More ominously, Garcon placed a red flag above the Union Jack that flew above the fort. Henceforward, quarter would be neither asked for nor given.

Meanwhile, Back in Spanish Pensacola

Governor Zuniga had commissioned twenty-five Black and mixed troops, along with two gunboats, to meet up with a band of Seminoles to capture Negro Fort. Zuniga had promised the Seminoles a set price for every captured and returned slave, along with trade goods and rum. (As would happen to the Americans over the next forty years, the Seminoles may have traded an empty promise for Spanish goods in order to buy time. Then again, maybe this particular branch of Seminoles had joined other slaves, freedmen and Indians on what promised to be a profitable slave hunting expedition.) The mixed force set sail from Pensacola. That same day, the U.S. Navy, the U.S. Army and Indian allies would bring the Battle of Negro Fort to a climactic and fiery conclusion.[220]

Negro Fort
July 27, 1816

The vice began to close on the multiracial fort, as the diverse coalition grew and exerted more pressure. The Negro Fort and the newly arrived U.S. gunboats exchanged ineffectual cannonades for an hour. And then it all ended in instantaneous, fiery oblivion when a preheated cannonball from a U.S. gunboat landed directly atop the fort's magazine.

The scene was eerily reminiscent of the explosion at Queen's Redoubt thirty-five years earlier. Dr. Marcus Buck, an eyewitness, described the carnage: "You cannot conceive, nor I describe the horrors of the scene. In an instant, hundreds of lifeless bodies were stretched upon the plain, buried in sand and rubbish, or suspended from the tops of the surrounding pines. Piles of bodies, large heaps of sand, broken guns, accoutrements, &c. covered the scite of the fort."[221]

The doctor and several soldiers began to cry. The American commander, Colonel Duncan Clinch, and most others rejoiced. Clinch thanked God for the slaughter: "The great Ruler of the Universe must have used us as his instrument in chastising the blood-thirsty & murderous wretches that defended the fort."[222]

The final casualty count at Negro Fort is difficult to tabulate. Some Maroons escaped before the battle began, while most of those wounded in the battle were mortally wounded. And so the casualty count continued to rise in the days after the explosion. In all, somewhere near two hundred Blacks and twenty-five Choctaw were killed by the lone cannonball.[223]

Further proof of the near annihilation of the defenders was that only twenty-five to fifty slaves were returned to their masters. The greatest slave hunting expedition in U.S. history had ended as a colossal failure. The Americans were left in possession of an utterly destroyed fort (in Spanish territory) and only two dozen slaves (most of whom belonged to Spanish citizens).

Ironically, Colonel Clinch was hailed as a hero. He had defeated the Black Maroon pirates with little loss himself. He had also displayed his courage and humanity in the battle's aftermath when he stopped McIntosh's warriors from massacring and scalping the survivors. (Of course, Clinch's "valor" in stopping the butchery was to preserve as many slaves as possible.)

Two of the few survivors were Garcon and the leader of the Choctaws. Garcon stumbled from the fort bloodied and blind but still defiant. McIntosh held an impromptu trial and promptly scalped and shot to death the two leaders of Negro Fort.[224]

The fort was destroyed. Most of its occupants were dead. And yet the struggle would continue. The resisting Indians received a dramatic and bloody reminder of what the United States was capable of in pursuit of land and slaves. Those slaves who survived death or capture fled inland to live in freedom and carry on the resistance alongside their Seminole allies. The United States' own Indian allies soon learned the futility of prostituting themselves to White slave hunters, as well as the even greater futility of aiding a nation intent on subjugating a continent under one master race, for most ended up in Indian Territory alongside the Seminoles. And finally, much of White America praised their heroes who had defeated a bloodthirsty and savage tribe and vanquished a colony of Maroons, likely preventing a bloody slave rebellion. But other White Americans saw the destruction of Negro Fort for what it was: a grand slave hunting expedition. In half a century, the two sides would battle it out for half a decade in the nation's deadliest war.

The Indians

December 28, 1835, Seventy Miles North of Tampa Bay
The Seminoles

Osceola crept through the foliage, undetected, his eyes on Fort King. The dilapidated and undermanned garrison was doomed unless the American relief party from Fort Brooke under Major Francis Langhorne Dade, one hundred miles to the south, arrived on time. But of course, the garrison could not know that the relief party, too, was doomed. Micanopy was on their trail.

Major Dade knew that trouble was brewing. Eerily reminiscent of the Creek strategy at Pensacola fifty-four years before—when the Indians had tormented the Spanish soldiers with war whoops, sniper attacks and unrelenting psychological warfare—the Seminoles likewise shadowed and serenaded Dade's men each day and night. Two days of broken sleep. Then three. Then four.

Dade's men marched, shivering in the cold morning dew. Micanopy's 180 warriors hid in the tall grass alongside the road. That same morning, the unsuspecting garrison also awoke to the chilled air. Osceola and a handful of braves lay well hidden in the dense brush outside the fort.

December 28, 1835, would begin a war, rouse one nation and ultimately send another into exile.

1814–1835

With the defeat of the Red Sticks in the southern United States in 1814, the defeated but unvanquished survivors of the Battle of Horseshoe Bend and

Osceola, chief of the Seminoles (circa 1900). *Beinecke Library at Yale University.*

other American encroachments fled to Spanish Florida. Many allied with local Florida tribes, and the "Seminole" people were born.

The Seminoles (sometimes translated as "renegade" or "Maroon") were a collection of various Indian tribes who had been fleeing White encroachment since the early 1700s. Occasionally, runaway slaves would join the communities of outcasts and freedom seekers. In 1817, influenced by the arrival of so many Creeks who had experience resisting Americans, many members of this new, confederated race of castoffs had grown tired of running. Most of the influential chiefs were determined to defend their homes. A guerrilla war—the First Seminole War—erupted and lasted until an uneasy peace between White settlers and the Seminoles was reached in 1823 when the Seminoles agreed to move farther south, into central Florida.[225]

One of the consequences of the First Seminole War was the destruction of Negro Fort. Just prior to the fort's demolition, some of the Black Maroons fled east and south, joining forces with other Seminole bands, thus strengthening the clout of the more martial chiefs. Unfortunately for the Seminoles, the presence of such a noticeable number of Blacks in the community caused the United States to blame the Indians for stealing slaves (property) from American citizens. Combined with the inevitable border raids by both sides and their concurrent atrocities, the fear of a slave insurrection (or even the existence of a Maroon colony within easy access to southern slave states) caused there to be a national outcry to punish the Seminoles. And so, the Second Seminole War erupted in 1835 with the goal of relocating every Florida Seminole to Indian Territory in Arkansas and returning every former slave to his or her owner.

The Dade Massacre

Major Dade must have breathed a sigh of relief as his two companies entered the pine and palmetto section of the trek. He had expected a Seminole attack in the thicker underbrush and the river crossings. But that treacherous landscape was now behind him. Fort King lay only twenty-five miles to the north. So confident was Dade in the imminent success of his march that he called in his flankers to the main unit. Dade's confidence trickled down into the ranks. Most of his soldiers kept their cartridge boxes under their buttoned coats, thus making quick access difficult. It didn't matter—they had passed the danger zone.

Ironically, Dade's soldiers were, to an extent, justified in their confidence. The Seminoles were no longer shadowing them—they were waiting for them in ambush.

The plan had been to await the arrival of Osceola. But Osceola was still hiding outside Fort King. With time running out, the Seminole chiefs held a counsel and decided to attack Dade's column despite the absence of Osceola.

The Pirates' Ruse Luring a Merchantman in the Olden Days (1896). *Library of Congress.*

A shot pierced the morning air, immediately followed by a volley that tore through the ranks of the blue-clad companies. Dozens fell, including Major Dade. The stunned Americans frantically prepared to defend themselves, while another and another and another Seminole volley decimated their ranks. With nowhere to flee, the terrified and desperate Americans made what stand they could. Using the scant materials at hand, the quickly diminishing survivors erected a barricade, hoping to hold off the Seminole warriors. They did. For six hours. And then only three remained, each presumed to be dead.

The Seminoles had won an unequivocal victory. They had wiped out two American companies of 103 men and lost only 3 themselves. The staggering defeat the Americans had inflicted on the British twenty-one years before at New Orleans the Seminole had now inflicted on the colossus to the north.[226]

Seminole Chief Tustenuggee (known to the Americans as "Chief Alligator") later related the events of that fateful day that would seal the fate of his people:

> *We had been preparing for this more than a year....Just as the day was breaking, we moved out of the swamp into the pine-barren. I counted, by*

144

The Indian War in Florida (1836). *Beinecke Library at Yale University.*

direction of Jumper, one hundred and eighty warriors. Upon approaching the road, each man chose his position on the west side....About nine o'clock in the morning the command approached....So soon as all the soldiers were opposite....Jumper gave the whoop, Micanopy fired the first rifle, the signal agreed upon, when every Indian arose and fired, which laid upon the ground, dead, more than half the white men. The cannon was discharged several times, but the men who loaded it were shot down as soon as the smoke cleared away....As we were returning to the swamp supposing all were dead, an Indian came up and said the white men were building a fort of logs. Jumper and myself, with ten warriors, returned. As we approached, we saw six men behind two logs placed one above another, with the cannon a short distance off....We soon came near, as the balls went over us. They had guns, but no powder, we looked in the boxes afterwards and found they were empty. The firing had ceased, and all was quiet when we returned to the swamp about noon. We left many negroes upon the ground looking at the dead men. Three warriors were killed and five wounded.[227]

Only three Americans survived the battle/massacre among the Florida palmettos. It was an unmitigated Seminole success. It was also the beginning of the end of the Florida Seminoles.

MEANWHILE, FORT KING'S INDIAN agent, Wiley Thompson, unwittingly left the fort with Lieutenant Constantine Smith for a stroll. Mirroring events twenty-five miles south, rifle fire pierced the air. Thompson fell with fourteen rifle bullets shredding his body. Lieutenant Smith likewise fell dead. So did the occupants of the sutler's cabin. Osceola plundered the cabin's goods and went to join Tustenuggee, Micanopy and the other chiefs to prepare to battle the dogs of war that their actions were sure to unleash.

When news of the attack on Dade's column spread, U.S. retaliation was swift and predictable—and, at first, largely ineffective. Seven years of insurgent warfare ensued. American military careers were made and destroyed. Hundreds died a warrior's death, and thousands more died of disease and starvation.

The Second Seminole War ended in 1842 with the forced relocation of most of the remaining Seminoles. A third and final war erupted in 1855 and lasted until 1858, when a war-weary United States and a handful of exhausted Seminoles simply stopped fighting. The last of the Florida Seminoles kept to the swamps, careful to avoid the Americans.

The three Seminole Wars would officially last a combined 15 years (although the standoff would go on for four decades), the United States' longest war in its nearly 250-year history. The wars captured the attention of the nation, galvanized racial attitudes in many and at the same time turned the Seminoles into mythic martyrs in the minds of others. On one side or the other, the majority of Americans had an opinion of the seemingly never-ending wars. More newspaper ink was devoted to the Seminole War after the Dade Massacre than to the Alamo and Texas War. Initially, most Americans sided against the Seminoles. Yet as the war(s) progressed, more and more began to question the conflict—both from fiscal and moral standpoints. Southerners tended to support the effort to eradicate a hostile tribe with numerous runaway Black slaves in its ranks. To northern states (and particularly the abolitionists), the war was nothing more than an attempt to extend slavery's borders.

A predictable pattern emerged throughout the course of the war. The U.S. Army, unable to defeat the Seminoles in a decisive battle, offered increasingly valuable inducements to encourage the Indians to move to Indian Territory in Arkansas. At first, the Indians were defiant. Then they realized the desperation of the Americans. Numerous chiefs would show up, accept the gifts and beg for more, telling the American commandant that they needed more gifts and time to convince their own people, hidden in the swamps, to relocate to Arkansas. Gifts in hand, the chiefs would then disappear, with enough food in tow for their people to survive another season.

By attrition and the hopelessness of the odds stacked against them, the Seminoles began to die or relocate by twos and threes and then dozens and scores. More and more accepted the American promise of a new homeland far to the west as the wars took their toll—in manpower, but mostly psychologically. Eventually, only a few holdouts remained.

After forty years, the Americans had finally conquered Florida, both West and East. By 1858, only about two hundred Seminoles remained, isolated in the southern tip. The rest of the unvanquished were repatriated to Indian Territory in Arkansas and Oklahoma.

John and Mary Lou Missall provided an interesting take on the three Seminole wars, which served as a microcosm for most of the United States' Indian wars:

> *At times it looks as if the motive for all this suffering was nothing more than greed. Yet what appears as greed to a far-removed observer would have been seen as simple survival to the nineteenth century citizens of whom we are being critical. Can we truly fault the common farmer who was struggling to raise enough grain to feed his family? Did he really want anything more than a better life for his children? And in that respect, was he really any different from us? Food on the table and a secure home are the two most basic of human needs. The solitary homesteader drove American expansion, and the vast majority of them were good, hard-working people. They simply wanted a better life.*[228]

While the Missalls are forgiving of the common American farmer, they are less so with the "peculiar institution." They blame slavery for the incessant American push into the southwest territories[229] and Spanish Florida. In their and other scholars' views, the Seminole Wars, like the expedition to Negro Fort, were nothing more than opportunistic slave hunting expeditions coupled with the desire to extend slavery from sea to sea and to the Gulf.

In the end, nearly every living Seminole ended up Indian Territory. And Florida entered the Union as a slave state.[230]

Chapter 13

THE END OF AN ERA, 1817–1820

THE RENEGADES

Galveztown, 1817–1820
The Brothers Laffite

With the destruction of their Barataria base, the Laffite brothers began to look for another site from which they could continue their smuggling operation. On account of recent revolutionary and filibustering turmoil in Mexico, the brothers decided to reopen business on Galveztown Island, just miles off the Texas Coast. The island was a small part of the seemingly never-ending territorial negotiations between the waning and waxing superpowers. Galveztown itself was thirty miles long, but only two to three miles in width. It had been named *Malhado* ("Ill-Fated") by early Spanish settlers and was inhabited by countless rattlesnakes and alligators. The only shade was a clump of trees in the center; the rest of the island was covered in sand, beach grass, scrub and sand dunes. Even the local Indians, the Karankawas, used the island only temporarily for fishing. And yet Galveztown had exactly what the brothers were looking for: an expansive harbor, just deep enough for smugglers and privateers but too shallow for more formidable ships that might be commissioned to destroy the former. In addition, the island lay in disputed territory on account of the various Mexican revolutions intent on overthrowing Spanish rule. (To further obscure the fate of Galveztown, where would the United States cast its die—with Spain or the revolutionaries?)[231]

In 1817, Jean sailed to his new headquarters in Galveztown, while Pierre continued to conduct business and supply the island from New Orleans. In turn, Galveztown began to launder its captured goods and, once again, supply the slave-hungry Americans of the Gulf Coast. As expected, a large percentage of the brothers' money still came from the illegal slave trade. Through privateering and piracy, the brothers began to realize a sizeable profit from their "Black Gold," in addition to their normal looted merchandise. Just as at Barataria, the pirated goods made their way to hungry markets, including New Orleans. (Jean's knowledge of the bayous into New Orleans continued to remain invaluable.) The brothers found an even safer way to dispose of their slaves by delivering the coffles right up to the border. American buyers would then pay one dollar per pound and smuggle the slaves into United States territory, thus taking the risk on themselves.[232]

It appeared that the move to Galveztown had been a wise decision for the brothers Laffite. However, two factors were working against Galveztown becoming the refuge they had known at Barataria (or even the pirate refuge Nassau had been a century before).

First, there was an international crackdown on piracy in general. (The insurance rate for merchantmen had recently jumped 100 percent.) Naturally, Spain was on the hunt for pirates, as His Most Catholic Majesty was the most affected by the corsairs of the Gulf. But the United States, too, was under pressure to eliminate pirates. Not only did its own merchants pay exorbitant insurance rates, but diplomatic negotiations for Florida also remained active. Piratical acts emanating from America threatened to stall those negotiations. Proof of the fledgling states' desire to eradicate piracy is evidenced by the dispatch of warships to the Gulf with orders to apprehend pirates. Several pirates were subsequently hanged along both U.S. coasts, Atlantic and the Gulf.[233]

The Laffite brothers were especially aware of the rising tide of anti-pirate sentiment. In Pierre's New Orleans, two men, Jean Desferges and Robert Johnson, were captured in the act of slave running and piracy. Even worse, one of Jean's associates on Galveztown, George Brown, led a raid on the American mainland at St. Landry Parish and held a prominent family at gunpoint while robbing them of their possessions, including ten slaves. Brown had broken one of the Laffites' preeminent rules: do not attack Americans. With retaliation certain to come, Jean captured Brown and had him hanged on a gallows overlooking the entrance to Galveztown so that all passing ships could testify to the fact that the Laffites did not tolerate piratical acts against Americans.[234]

Secondly, after years of tension over the Mississippi River, East and West Florida, the disputed borderlands between Texas and Louisiana and the exact location of Spain's northern border, the two nations had hammered out a treaty that was expected to be ratified imminently.[235] Upon ratification, the United States would be expected to punish any and all (U.S. citizens or not) who used U.S. land as a staging point for raids on Spanish lands or shipping. With stricter laws being enforced more stringently and with American warships in the Gulf to do the enforcing, the Laffite brothers realized that they were operating from Galveztown on borrowed time. It was time to relocate.[236]

Pierre began to search for another base. Soon Jean joined his brother in New Orleans, where it quickly became apparent to both that the celebrity they had enjoyed in the afterglow of the Battle of New Orleans had dimmed considerably. With their smuggling empire collapsing, their finances quickly dwindling and soon to be homeless, the brothers decided to roll the die. On January 3, 1820, Pierre wrote a letter to Commodore Daniel Patterson:

> *Too long since the names of the Lafittes have been the object of general execration, as well here as abroad....To shew the whole world that I never contributed to the violation of the sacred rights of nations, or would offer resistance or offense to the Government of the United States;... and to destroy all fears which the Establishment of Galveztown might occasion;...I now offer myself to you, Sir, willingly, and at my own risk and expense, to Clear Galveztown, and disband all those which are to be found there; taking the engagement for myself and my Brother, that it shall never serve as a place of Rendez-vous for any undertakings with our consent, or under our authorization.*[237]

Although Patterson did not trust the Laffite brothers, he agreed to Pierre's proposal. In exchange for destroying the pirates' nest at Galveztown, the Laffites would receive a safe conduct pass to remove their own personal ships, supplies and men to a territory outside U.S. jurisdiction. Patterson wrote to a comrade that he had authorized the brothers to take care of the Galveztown problem: "[T]he *residences, buildings* &c. there erected, shall be razed to the ground, that every means shall be removed from thence which has hitherto rendered it the retreat and security of [the pirate] Aury and others who have from thence preyed upon the commerce of the Gulf of Mexico."[238]

In January 1820, Jean and Pierre parted—Jean for Galveztown, Pierre to remain in New Orleans with plans to join his brother later. Neither knew that this would be their final parting. True to his promise, Jean arrived at Galveztown and set fire to all the buildings, save a few set aside for his men as they continued to cleanse the island. The earthworks were dismantled, and ships that Jean did not plan to convoy with him to his new abode were burned. The younger Laffite seemed to be keeping his word. But still, he remained on the island. Patterson kept urging him to wrap up his operation and leave promptly. Jean remained. Pierre, hoping to join his brother, was delayed. The brothers were pushing the patience of the United States.

Finally, on May 7, 1820, Jean left Galveztown for good. He allowed those on the island to make their own choice: remain on the island and take their chances or accompany him on his next quest. The response was mixed:

> *When the little squadron of three vessels lifted anchor and sailed through the pass and out into the Gulf, the spires of smoke fading in the distance behind them testified not only to the ashes of Galveston, but to the ruination of all that Jean and Pierre Laffite had tried to achieve for a decade. They were cast out to sea by a failed past and about to face an uncertain future.*[239]

Those who chose to sail with Jean Laffite sailed to their doom. Never again would he return to the land that had made him a legend.[240]

May 24, 1820
New Orleans

Jean Desfarges and his lieutenant, Robert Johnson, pirates based out of Galveztown, had been captured and convicted of piracy and slave running. When the day of their hanging arrived, the two were brought to the wharf to the delight of a rowdy New Orleans crowd eager for entertainment and blood. Standing atop a barge and beneath the noose, Desfarges asked his executioner for a pistol so he could shoot himself. When refused, the pirate—still bound in handcuffs—leaped into the Gulf, hoping to die at sea. Alert sailors "rescued" Desfarges and promptly hanged him and his comrade from the gallows.[241]

November 9, 1821
Telyas, Yucatan

Pierre and his latest lover, Lucia Allen, entered the tiny village of Telyas on the Yucatan Peninsula. The elder pirate had been wounded a week before when Spanish soldiers attacked and nearly captured the outlaw on the island of Cancun. Even worse, Pierre was suffering from a severe fever. For three days, the fever raged as less than a handful of loyal pirates and his lover tended him. William C. Davis related:

> *Then, on or about November 9, within sight and sound of thousands of pink flamingos feeding in the lagoon, Pierre Laffite breathed his last. He died the pirate he always claimed he never was, and though he escaped the noose or bullet that would have been his fate if captured, his death was the direct result of his trade.*[242]

Pierre's men buried him at the Catholic church of Santa Clara of Dzidzantun on the Yucatan Peninsula.[243]

House on Ellicott's Hill, Natchez, Mississippi. *Collection of Ryan Starrett.*

February 4, 1823
Gulf of Honduras

As dawn rose, Jean Laffite, aboard his ship, *General Santander*, noticed two ships, a brigantine and schooner, sailing in the distance. When the ships noticed Laffite, they fled. Jean spent the next seventeen hours running down the brigantine, assuming that it was a Spanish merchantman. When at last he caught up, the brigantine turned and fired on the pirate, simultaneously signaling for the schooner to join the fray. The last of the Laffites had made a fatal miscalculation.

Outgunned, the desperate pirates fought back. Night fell, and cannon fire illuminated the skies. The trio exchanged shots into the early morning hours, when Jean was struck by either grape shot or the shrapnel of wooden splinters. The wound was serious enough that Jean handed command over to his lieutenant. Still, Jean encouraged his men as they fought imminent death—or a delayed death if captured. Finally, sometime after one o'clock in the morning, *General Santander* limped away from the fray.

Several hours later, Jean Laffite died of his wounds. His men placed his body in the Gulf of Mexico, the Gulf that he had made his home.[244]

America's most famous pirate died a pirate's death.

EPILOGUE

Yes, I am a pirate, two hundred years too late
The cannons don't thunder, there's nothin' to plunder
I'm an over-forty victim of fate
Arriving too late, arriving too late
...
My occupational hazard being my occupation's just not around[245]

ast-forward two hundred years. The Gulf Coast's most famous pirate has earned hundreds of millions of dollars in record sales, concerts, resorts and restaurants all along the Gulf Coast. As the first quarter of the twenty-first century comes to a close, Parrotheads keep the Pirate King on the throne into his eighth decade—an impressive feat given the brief careers of those who previously sought hegemony of the coast.

The Gulf Coast has always been a refuge for pirates, renegades and outliers. From the colonial French adventurers to the Kaintucks; from Al Capone's Ocean Springs operation to the Dixie Mafia; from Jean Guilhot, the Hermit of Deer Island, to the eccentric and brilliant Walter Anderson; from George Ohr, the "Mad Potter," to the "Son of a Son of a Sailor" from Pascagoula, those who lived on the edge—culturally and legally (and sometimes both)—have always been welcomed to the land of misfits.

From the Redneck Riviera to Shearwater Pottery in Ocean Springs to Fishbone Alley in Gulfport to Frenchmen and Bourbon Street, the Gulf Coast still offers a safe refuge for the "cultural infidels" and renegades of the twenty-first century.

Above: Jimmy Buffett takes part in a U.S. Naval Academy cruise in 2016. *U.S. Naval Academy.*

Left: A pair of pirates at Bay St. Louis Pirate Day, 2022. *Collection of Ryan Starrett.*

A master of marketing, Jimmy Buffett understands mankind's innate sense of nostalgia and escapism. One need look no further than the turnout at the annual pirate festivals all along the coast. The desire to be pirate for a day, to live in the age of raiders, invaders and pirates of the Gulf Coast, still resonates to this day.

NOTES

Introduction

1. And thus, the historic site of Juneteenth.
2. Worsham, "Jefferson Looks Westward."

Chapter 1

3. D'Iberville, *Iberville's Gulf Journals*, 133.
4. Ibid., 170.
5. Gilles Havard suggests that rather than learning multiple Indian languages, Bienville had learned Mobilian, which served as the *lingua franca* of the Gulf Coast. Thus, he was able to interpret and speak with several different tribes.
6. D'Iberville, *Iberville's Gulf Journals*, 172–73.
7. Ibid., 172.
8. Ibid., 173.
9. Ibid.
10. Even in the White Earth/Apple village itself, there was strife with some villagers siding with Oyelape (the second ranking chief) on the side of the British and some with the French, including the ranking chief Old Hair, who was currently in Bienville's island prison.

11. Penicaut, *Fleur de Lys and Calumet*, 176.
12. Mitchell, *New History of Mississippi*, 17.
13. Barnett, *Natchez Indians*, 67–68.
14. Peace pipe.
15. Penicaut, *Fleur de Lys and Calumet*, 181.
16. The French had anticipated the efficacy of the fingerprint by nearly two hundred years.
17. Ibid., 177–81, and Mitchell, *New History of Mississippi*, 18.
18. Barnett, *Natchez Indians*, 71.
19. The entirety of the Natchez War of 1714—albeit from the French point of view—can be found in Penicaut, *Fleur de Lys and Calumet*, 166–82.
20. Most likely rum or homemade moonshine.
21. Ladnier, "Jean Baptiste and Henriette," 21.
22. Ibid., 22.
23. Ibid., 23.
24. Ibid., 28–30.
25. Ibid., 31.
26. Henriette ended up marrying the Mobile church warden. Her and Jean Baptiste's second child was born during their elopement to Havana.
27. Ladnier, "Jean Baptiste and Henriette," 37, 40.
28. Ibid., 37.
29. Ibid., 43.
30. Ibid., 49.
31. Ibid., 53–54.
32. Ibid., 59.
33. Ibid. The trial of Jean Baptiste is controversial. The Swiss deserters had provided Jean Baptiste with a letter claiming that he had had no part in the murder and had been forced to serve the deserters as a guide. The court, however, decided otherwise, believing him to be an integral part of the plot. The story here adheres to the scholarship of Randal Ladnier and presents Jean Baptiste as an accomplice to murder. However, the authors concede that there is an alternate interpretation and that Jean Baptiste might have been wrongfully executed. The authors also highly recommend Eloise Genest's excellent historical novel, *The Passions of Princes*, which deals with the life and times of Jean Baptiste Baudreau II.

Chapter 2

34. The famed Frenchman Street received its name when six Frenchmen were executed for attempting to lead a rebellion against the Spanish takeover in 1769.
35. DuVal, *Independence Lost*, 121.
36. Caughey, *Bernardo de Galvez in Louisiana*, 63.
37. Ibid., 65.
38. Ibid., 152–53.
39. Saravia, *Bernardo de Gálvez*, 140–47.
40. Ibid., 147.
41. Caughey, *Bernardo de Galvez in Louisiana*, 150.
42. Ibid., 163.
43. Fleming, "Bernardo de Galvez," 154–55.
44. DuVal, *Independence Lost*, 149.
45. Galvez's Mississippi campaign can be found in Fleming, "Bernardo de Galvez"; Caughey, *Bernardo de Galvez in Louisiana*, 154–58; and DuVal, *Independence Lost*, 147–51.
46. Caughey, *Bernardo de Galvez in Louisiana*, 171.
47. Because of storms, difficult sailing and problems entering the bay, it took Galvez more than a month to land outside Fort Charlotte.
48. Caughey, *Bernardo de Galvez in Louisiana*, 180–81, and DuVal, *Independence Lost*, 170–71.
49. This redoubt was built on the highest hill overlooking the city of Pensacola. It also hovered over Fort George. If captured by the Spanish, holding the fort and the city would be untenable.
50. Bowles likely received a commission at such a young age through family connections. Nevertheless, Bowles was a committed British soldier throughout 1777–78 and was a participant at the Battle of Monmouth.
51. Once again, "Muskogee" and "Creek" are interchangeable in the present chapter.
52. Bowles sired at least two Creek children. Under Creek law and its matrilineal laws of succession, the children would have "belonged" to his wife's family, making the two "full-blooded" Creek.
53. Wright, *William Augustus Bowles*, 14.
54. Prior to the May 8 disaster, Bowles did sally forth with his unit and take the Spanish by surprise as they took cover from British cannon fire (although the latter shots carried no balls to allow the British to sneak up on the Spanish trench). Bowles and company put nineteen Spaniards to the bayonet and temporarily delayed the fall of Pensacola.

55. Philbrick, *In the Hurricane's Eye*, 10–18.
56. DuVal, *Independence Lost*, 188–89. For more information on the hurricanes of 1780, see Philbrick, *In the Hurricane's Eye* (pages 10–18 are a must).
57. Richard Bell, "The American Revolution in the Caribbean: The Untold Story Lecture," March 14, 2022, Smithsonian Associates.
58. In addition to fighting on the North American mainland and West Indies, Britain was also invested in defending Nicaragua (from Galvez's father), Honduras and Gibraltar. The American Revolutionary War was truly a world war.
59. Caughey, *Bernardo de Galvez in Louisiana*, 203.
60. Ibid.
61. Technically, the Siege of Pensacola took place from March 9, 1781, to May 8, 1781, making it the longest siege of the American Revolutionary War (unless one includes the Siege of Gibraltar).
62. DuVal, *Independence Lost*, 199.
63. Ibid., 206.
64. American Battlefield Trust, "Pensacola March."
65. DuVal, *Independence Lost*, 200–201.
66. Ibid., 213.
67. Caughey, *Bernardo de Galvez in Louisiana*, 214.

Chapter 3

68. James, *Black Jacobins*, 87.
69. Sublette, *World that Made New Orleans*, 152.
70. Rasmussen, *American Uprising*, 44.
71. Sublette, *World that Made New Orleans*, 153.
72. Rasmussen, *American Uprising*, 44.
73. Foreman, "History of the United States' First Refugee Crisis." More than twenty-five thousand refugees fled the revolution. Many ended up in Central or South America or on other Caribbean islands.
74. Saxon, *Lafitte the Pirate*, 152–53.
75. James, *Black Jacobins*, 32.
76. Saxon, *Lafitte the Pirate*, 179.
77. Allende, *Island Beneath the Sea*, 314.
78. Rice, *Feast of All Saints*, 528.
79. Davis, *Pirates Laffite*, 11.
80. Foreman, "History of the United States' First Refugee Crisis."

81. Ibid.
82. William Shakespeare, *Mark Antony*, Act III, Scene I, Line 273.

Chapter 4

83. Members of the Continental Congress and Continental army became upset when they learned the exact terms of the British surrender to Galvez. The Spaniard had allowed the Redcoats to sail to New York, where they would stay until formally paroled in a prisoner exchange. In the meantime, they took an oath not to fight against any Spanish forces for the duration of the war. Galvez (through foresight or negligence) did not make them take an oath against fighting American troops. (After all, according to Spain, there was no "United States of America"—only a rebellious people engaged in a civil war with their mother country. Spain was in the precarious position of supporting colonials against their mother country, while it was a colonial superpower itself. The potential ramifications of such support was not lost on Spain. Hence, throughout the war, Spain would attack British outposts but never formally ally with or recognize American independence.) Now, those captured British soldiers were free to continue their fight against American/rebel troops. And they were sent right across the river from George Washington's troops. In effect, Galvez had taken Pensacola but sent his prisoners to the spot where America least wanted to see them. And he kept the valuable port for the king of Spain.

84. The Panton, Leslie & Company empire stretched from the Bahamas to New Orleans and up to Memphis. It served the Creeks, Seminoles, Chickasaws, Choctaws and Cherokees.

85. One of the reasons William Augustus Bowles failed to unite all the Creek villages was McGillivray's own charisma and insistence on remaining loyal to Spain—and by extension, Panton, Leslie & Company.

86. Din, *War on the Gulf Coast*, 85.

87. Wright, *William Augustus Bowles*, 66.

88. St. Marks Fort in St. Marks, Florida.

89. Din, *War on the Gulf Coast*, 46–47, 60. The irony of Cunningham ending up in the Philippines—and dying there—will be evident momentarily.

90. The man who first captured the "Director-General" was New Orleans port master and captain Jose de Helvia. Helvia was responsible for capturing the British ship bringing supplies to Manchac—Galvez's first

Gulf Coast conquest. He was also with Galvez during the capture of Mobile in 1780. See Holmes, "Evia, Jose Antonio de."

91. Din, *War on the Gulf Coast*, 45.

92. Wright, *William Augustus Bowles*, 66–70.

93. Ibid., 94.

94. Din, *War on the Gulf Coast*, 60–61.

95. Wright, *William Augustus Bowles*, 95–106.

96. Din, *War on the Gulf Coast*, 82–84.

97. Wright, *William Augustus Bowles*, 115–16.

98. Ibid., 118.

99. Fort St. Marks in St. Marks, Florida.

100. Wright, *William Augustus Bowles*, 127.

101. Ibid., 128–31.

102. McAlister, "William Augustus Bowles."

103. Ibid.

Chapter 5

104. Alford, *Prince Among Slaves*, 22.

105. Ibid.

106. An African slave trader.

107. Alford, *Prince Among Slaves*, 23.

108. Ibid.

109. Ibid.

110. A subgroup of the Yoruba people.

111. Hurston, *Barracoon*, 51–52.

112. UNESCO—Slavery and Remembrance, "Ouidah."

113. Hurston, *Barracoon*, 53–54.

114. The *Clotilda* was the last known slave ship to enter the United States. The ship arrived in Mobile, carrying 110 African slaves just before the onset of the American Civil War.

115. Alford, *Prince Among Slaves*, 34–35.

116. Rasmussen, *American Uprising*, 23.

117. Tanner, *Chained to the Land*, 169.

118. The *Clotilda*, the last known slave ship in the United States, entered Mobile Bay with its illegal cargo/humans in 1860.

Chapter 6

119. *Green Mountain Patriot*, "Gun-Boat No. 3—Taken!," August 20, 1805.
120. Editorial, *Mississippi Messenger*, September 20, 1805.
121. Louisiana: European Explorations and the Louisiana Purchase, a special presentation from the Geography and Map Division of the Library of Congress, https://www.loc.gov/static/collections/louisiana-european explorations-and-the-louisiana-purchase/images/lapurchase.pdf.
122. Eric Herschthal, "Slaves, Spaniards, and Subversion in Early Louisiana: The Persistent Fears of Black Revolt and Spanish Collusion in Territorial Louisiana, 1803–1812," *Journal of the Early Republic* 36, no. 2 (2016).
123. Present-day Alabama.
124. Wright, *William Augustus Bowles*, 166–67.
125. Among the captors were Sam Moniac and Charles Weatherford.
126. Wright, *William Augustus Bowles*, 167–68.
127. Ibid., 169.
128. Some scholars suggest that Spanish guards systematically starved Bowles. Others suggest that in a fit of despair and depression, the director-general starved himself. One way or another, it was an inglorious end to such an adventurous career.
129. Present-day West Feliciana Parish.
130. Davis, *Rogue Republic*, 30.
131. Ibid., 51–52.
132. An excellent account of the Kempers' first attempt to wrest control of Baton Rouge from the Spanish can be found in Davis, *Rogue Republic*, 38–52. The vignette here is taken entirely from Davis's work. The authors highly recommend reading *The Rogue Republic* for the definitive story of the West Florida Republic. As to the Kemper brothers, Samuel would continue his fight against Spain by joining Mexican revolutionaries in the failed Gutierrez-Magee Expedition. Reuben joined the 1810 rebellion, where he made a failed attempt to capture Mobile from Spain. He, too, joined the disastrous Gutierrez-Magee Expedition and later fought under Andrew Jackson at the Battle of New Orleans. Near the end of an active and tumultuous life, Reuben Kemper finally settled down as a planter in Mississippi and died in Natchez in 1827.
133. Davis, *Rogue Republic*, 120.
134. Ibid., 181.
135. Ibid., 184.

136. The entire battle for Fort San Carlos can be found in Davis, *Rogue Republic*, 172–87.

Chapter 7

137. Rasmussen, *American Uprising*, 135.
138. Ibid., 102.
139. Ibid., 106.
140. Kook is referred to as a giant because he stood over six feet tall. The average slave at the time stood five feet, three and a half inches tall. Rasmussen, *American Uprising*, 106 and 108–9.
141. Rasmussen, *American Uprising*, 126.
142. Ibid., 139–40.
143. Ibid., 140.
144. Ibid., 140–42.
145. Ibid., 156.
146. Ibid., 157.

Chapter 8

147. Davis, *Pirates Laffite*, 38.
148. Ibid., 50–52.
149. Ibid., 42.
150. Ibid., 43.
151. Ibid., 52.
152. Ibid., 57.
153. Ibid., 58.
154. Ibid., 76.

Chapter 9

155. *Alexandria Gazette*, "Good News-Mobile Taken!," May 29, 1813 (originally published in the *Mobile Gazette*).
156. *Alexandria Gazette*, "The Eyes of the Nation Will Be Diverted…," May 29, 1813.
157. Mixed race, White and Indian (in Bailey's case, White and Creek).

158. South Alabama.
159. Waselkov, *Conquering Spirit*, 54.
160. Mims's wells still provided water inside the fort, but they were now covered by Red Stick musket fire. Anyone daring to quench their thirst had to run a gauntlet of bullets and arrows.
161. Waselkov, *Conquering Spirit*, 196.
162. An excellent account of the Battle of Fort Mims can be found in Waselkov, *Conquering Spirit*, 116–38. The account here comes almost exclusively from Waselkov's definitive history of the battle.
163. Crockett, *King of the Wild Frontier*, 56.
164. Ibid.
165. Ibid., 57.
166. Ibid., 64.
167. Ibid., 65.
168. Ibid., 66.
169. Ibid., 69.
170. Ibid., 71–72.
171. Ibid., 74.

Chapter 10

172. Davis, *Pirates Laffite*, 158.
173. Ibid., 165–74.
174. Ibid., 175.
175. Ibid., 185–87.
176. Ibid., 186.
177. Ibid., 186–89.
178. CPI Inflation Calculator.
179. Davis, *Pirates Laffite*, 190–95.
180. Ibid., 208–9.

Chapter 11

181. George Robert Gleig wrote of using fir apples as projectiles in the British army's pretend war on Dauphin Island following the Battle of New Orleans. The authors, however, cannot find evidence of fir apple potatoes growing on the island (although it would not be the first printed mistake

made by said authors). Regardless of the claimed natural missile—be it tuber, spud or the simple but effective pinecone—His Majesty's Army no doubt engaged in a civil war on Dauphin Island with the intention of releasing stress and alleviating boredom.

182. Gleig, *Campaigns of the British Army*, 189.

183. For the Battle of New Orleans casualty count, see Davis, *Greatest Fury*, 278.

184. Davis, *Greatest Fury*, 228.

185. Gleig, *Campaigns of the British Army*, 142–43; and Davis, *Greatest Fury*, 82–83.

186. Gleig, *Campaigns of the British Army*, 143.

187. Ibid., 143.

188. Ibid., 148.

189. Ibid.

190. Ibid., 150–51.

191. Ibid., 153–54.

192. Ibid., 155.

193. Ibid., 156.

194. Ibid., 155.

195. Ibid., 155–56.

196. Kilmeade and Yaeger, *Andrew Jackson and the Miracle of New Orleans*, 173.

197. Ibid., 180.

198. Gleig, *Campaigns of the British Army*, 169.

199. Kilmeade and Yaeger, *Andrew Jackson and the Miracle of New Orleans*, 180–83.

200. Gleig, *Campaigns of the British Army*, 171.

201. Kilmeade and Yaeger, *Andrew Jackson and the Miracle of New Orleans*, 190–91.

202. Gleig, *Campaigns of the British Army*, 175.

203. Davis, *Greatest Fury*, 278.

204. Ibid., 279.

205. Ibid., 297.

206. Gleig, *Campaigns of the British Army*, 151.

207. Ibid., 189.

Chapter 12

208. Clavin, *Battle of Negro Fort*, 83–84.

209. Modern-day Apalachicola, Florida.

210. Clavin, *Battle of Negro Fort*, 85–86.

211. Ibid., 85–90.
212. Ibid., 93–94.
213. Ibid., 107.
214. Ibid., 110.
215. Ibid., 109.
216. Ibid., 108.
217. Ibid., 114–15.
218. Ibid., 115–16.
219. Ibid., 118–19.
220. Ibid., 120.
221. Ibid., 122.
222. Ibid.
223. Ibid., 123.
224. Ibid., 124.
225. Although the Treaty of Moultrie Creek was not signed until 1823, fighting had all but ceased by 1818, making the First Seminole War the briefest of the three.
226. Missall and Missall, *Seminole Wars*, 96.
227. Barr, *Correct and Authentic Narrative*.
228. Missall and Missall, *Seminole Wars*, 222.
229. Present-day Alabama, Mississippi and parts of Louisiana.
230. John and Mary Lou Missall propose another interesting take on the culpability for Seminole removal: "If we want to blame anyone, we might start with the person who stares back at us when we look in the mirror. How many of us live in homes that stand on land that once belonged to an Indian nation?…In the end, we all share a small portion of the responsibility for what happened to the Seminoles and other native peoples. We cannot, however, go back and change the past or make it go away. The best we can do is work to see that it does not happen again. Justice, equality, and tolerance will always be 'works in progress.'" Missall and Missall, *Seminole Wars*, 223. Almost the entirety of the vignette here on the Seminole Wars comes from the Missalls' tome. The authors highly recommend the fascinating read.

Chapter 13

231. Davis, *Pirates Laffite*, 302.
232. Ibid., 362.

233. Ibid., 419.
234. Ibid., 420.
235. The Adams-Onis Treaty formally handed Florida over to the United States.
236. Davis, *Pirates Laffite*, 419.
237. Ibid., 421–22.
238. Ibid., 424.
239. Ibid., 432.
240. The fate of Jean Laffite is uncertain. The following addendum to Laffite's career is based on the scholarship of the preeminent Laffite scholar William C. Davis.
241. Davis, *Pirates Laffite*, 434.
242. Ibid., 454.
243. Ibid.
244. Ibid., 462–63.

Epilogue

245. Jimmy Buffett, "A Pirate Looks at Forty," lyrics © Duchess Music Corporation.

SOURCES

Articles

Fleming, Thomas. "Bernardo de Galvez." *American Heritage* 3, no. 3 (April/
    May 1982).
Foreman, Nicholas. "The History of the United States' First Refugee Crisis."
    Smithsonian Magazine (January 5, 2016).
Ladnier, Randall. "Jean Baptiste and Henriette: A Creole Tragedy." *Jackson
    County Historical and Genealogical Society Journal* 19 (2020).
McAlister, Lyle N. "William Augustus Bowles and the State of Muskogee."
    Florida Historical Quarterly (n.d.): 326.

Books

Alford, Terry. *Prince Among Slaves: The True Story of an African Prince Sold Into
    Slavery in the American South*. Oxford, UK: Oxford University Press, 2007.
Allende, Isabel. *Island Beneath the Sea*. New York: Harper Collins, 2010.
Barnett, James F., Jr. *The Natchez Indians: A History to 1735*. Jackson: University
    Press of Mississippi, 2007.
Barr, James, Captain. *Correct and Authentic Narrative of the Indian War in Florida,
    with a Description of Maj. Dade's Massacre, and an Account of the Extreme Suffering,
    for Want of Provisions, of the Army-Having Been Obliged to Eat Horses' and Dogs'
    Flesh, etc*. New York: J. Narine, Printer, 1836.

Buffett, Jimmy. *A Pirate Looks at Fifty*. New York: Ballantine Books, 1998.

Caughey, John Walton. *Bernardo de Galvez in Louisiana, 1776–1784*. Louisiana Parish Historical Series. Gretna, LA: Pelican Publishing, 1998.

Clavin, Matthew J. *The Battle of Negro Fort: The Rise and Fall of a Fugitive Slave Community*. New York: New York University Press, 2019.

Crockett, Davy. *King of the Wild Frontier*. Mineola, NY: Dover Publications Inc., 2010.

Davis, William C. *The Greatest Fury: The Battle of New Orleans and the Rebirth of America*. New York: Penguin Random House, 2019.

———. *The Pirates Laffite: The Treacherous World of the Corsairs of the Gulf*. Orlando, FL: Harcourt Inc., 2005.

———. *The Rogue Republic: How Would-Be Patriots Waged the Shortest Revolution in American History*. New York: Houghton Mifflin Harcourt, 2011.

D'Iberville, Pierre Le Moyne. *Iberville's Gulf Journals*. Translated by Richebourg Gaillard McWilliams. Tuscaloosa: University of Alabama Press, 1981.

Din, Gilbert C. *War on the Gulf Coast: The Spanish Fight Against William Augustus Bowles*. Gainesville: University of Florida Press, 2012.

DuVal, Kathleen. *Independence Lost: Lives on the Edge of the American Revolution*. New York: Random House, 2015.

Gleig, George Robert. *The Campaigns of the British Army at Washington and New Orleans, in the Years 1814–1815*. London: John Murray, n.d.

Hurston, Zora Neale. *Barracoon: The Story of the Last "Black Cargo."* New York: Amistad, 2018.

James, C.L.R. *The Black Jacobins: Toussaint L'Ouverture and the Santo Domingo Revolution*. New York: Vintage Books, 1989.

Kilmeade, Brian, and Don Yaeger. *Andrew Jackson and the Miracle of New Orleans: The Battle that Shaped America's Destiny*. New York: Penguin Random House, 2017.

Missall, John, and Mary Lou Missall. *The Seminole Wars: America's Longest Indian Conflict*. Gainesville: University Press of Florida, 2004.

Mitchell, Dennis J. *A New History of Mississippi*. Jackson: University Press of Mississippi, 2014.

Penicaut, Andre. *Fleur de Lys and Calumet: Being the Penicaut Narrative of French Adventure in Louisiana*. Translated by Richebourg Gaillard McWilliams. Tuscaloosa: University of Alabama Press, 1953.

Philbrick, Nathaniel. *In The Hurricane's Eye: The Genius of George Washington and the Victory at Yorktown*. New York: Viking, 2018.

Rasmussen, Daniel. *American Uprising: The Untold Story of America's Largest Slave Revolt*. New York: Harper Perennial, 2011.

Rice, Anne. *The Feast of All Saints*. New York: Ballantine Books, 1979.

Saravia, Gonzalo M. Qunitero. *Bernardo de Gálvez: Spanish Hero of the American Revolution*. Chapel Hill: University of North Carolina Press, 2018.

Saxon, Lyle. *Lafitte the Pirate*. Gretna, LA: Pelican Publishing, 1999.

Sublette, Ned. *The World that Made New Orleans: From Spanish Silver to Congo Square*. Chicago: Lawrence Hill, 2009.

Tanner, Lynette Ater, ed. *Chained to the Land: Vices from Cotton & Cane Plantations*. Winston-Salem, NC: John F. Blair, Publisher, 2014.

Waselkov, Gregory A. *A Conquering Spirit: Fort Mims and the Redstick War of 1813–1814*. Tuscaloosa: University of Alabama Press, 2006.

Wright, J. Leitch, Jr. *William Augustus Bowles: Director General of the Creek Nation*. Athens: University of Georgia Press, 1967.

Internet

American Battlefield Trust. "Pensacola March 9–May 10, 1781." https://www.battlefields.org/learn/maps/pensacola-march-9-may-10-1781.

CPI Inflation Calculator. https://www.officialdata.org/us/inflation/1810?amount=1000000.

Havard, Gilles. "Jean-Baptiste Le Moyne De Bienville." Bibliothcue Nationale De France. https://heritage.bnf.fr/france-ameriques/en/bienville-article.

Holmes, Jack D.L. "Evia, Jose Antonio de." Texas State Historical Association. https://www.tshaonline.org/handbook/entries/evia-jose-antonio-de.

UNESCO—Slavery and Remembrance. "Ouidah." http://slaveryandremembrance.org/articles/article/?id=A0120.

Worsham, James. "Jefferson Looks Westward: President Secretly Sought Funds from Congress to Explore Louisiana Territory, Develop Trade." *Prologue* 34, no. 4 (Winter 2002). National Archives. https://www.archives.gov/publications/prologue/2002/winter/jefferson-message.html.

ABOUT THE AUTHORS

RYAN STARRETT was birthed and reared in Jackson, Mississippi. After receiving degrees from the University of Dallas, Adams State University and Spring Hill College, as well as spending a ten-year hiatus in Texas, he returned home to continue his teaching career. He lives in Madison with his wife, Jackie, and two children, Joseph Padraic and Penelope Rose O.

JOSH FOREMAN was born and raised in the Jackson Metro Area. He is a sixth-generation Mississippian and an eleventh-generation southerner. He lived, taught and wrote in South Korea from 2005 to 2014. He holds degrees from Mississippi State University and the University of New Hampshire. He lives in Starkville, Mississippi, with his wife, Melissa, and his three children, Keeland, Genevieve and Ulrich.